The Civil War In Missouri

As Seen From The Capital City

By

Dino A. Brugioni

Pictorial Concept by Joseph S. Summers, Jr.

COVER PHOTO: General John C. Fremont arrived in Jefferson City shortly after the Battle of Lexington in September 1861. This October 19, 1861, *Harper's Weekly* sketch shows the arrival of troops and the construction of fortifications.

(State Historical Society of Missouri)

Summers Publishing
515 E. High Street
Jefferson City, Missouri 65101

Printed in the United States of America

Library of Congress Catalog Card Number:
86-71353

ISBN 0-916109-05-4

Contents

Introduction

In 1860, Missouri was the gateway to the west. The burgeoning railroad lines, the Missouri River and its tributaries, and the rumbling stagecoaches that trundled over a primitive network of roads offered the adventurous pioneer access to destinations across the western frontier. Missouri was, indeed, of great importance to the North.

How could Missouri, a wealthy slave state and the only slave-holding border state west of the Mississippi River, remain in the Union with a governor, lieutenant governor and a large portion of the legislature favoring secession?

How could Jefferson City, the seat of government of a divided state, survive with minimal damage?

The official records of the federal government, *A Compendium of the War of the Rebellion*, lists 882 battles, engagements, actions, skirmishes, and affairs on Missouri soil, some within sight of the state capital. Only Virginia and Tennessee saw more. Hostilities were intensified by Southern sympathizing renegades under no direct control of the Confederate states. Who were these bearers of terror and misery?

These answers and events are clearly related by Dino A. Brugioni in this excellent review of the Civil War as seen from Jefferson City.

Joseph S. Summers, Jr.

Acknowledgments

While researching and writing this book, I was encouraged by many, and have incurred substantial debt to them for their time, patience and experience. Therefore, grateful acknowledgment is here made: To the many sources referenced in the Bibliography. Without them, the book would not have been possible.

To Dr. Joseph S. Summers, Jr., who encouraged the publication of this book, for his loyalty and devotion, and for his self-sacrificing expenditure of patience, time and funds to have the book published.

To the management of the *Jefferson City News Tribune* for their permission to use information from the July 1985 articles I wrote and which appeared in their newspaper.

To the staffs of the following divisions of the Library of Congress: The Rare Book and Special Collection Division for making available rare historical books and materials on Jefferson City and Missouri during the Civil War; the Prints and Photographs Division for photos of the period; the General Reading Rooms Division, for making available reference materials on Jefferson City; and to John Wolter, the Chief of the Geography and Map Division for providing maps and sketches of Jefferson City.

To the staff of the Central Information Division of the National Archives and Records Administration, and to John E. Taylor of the Cartographic and Architectural Branch for making available maps of Jefferson City created during the Civil War.

To the staff of the Department of Memorial Affairs of the Veterans Administration, and especially to Dorothy Vrazke of the Cemetery Service for providing information on the Centralia Raid and the Jefferson City National Cemetery.

To the State Historical Society of Missouri for information and many of the photographs in this publication.

To Robert F. McCort for his advice and editing of the original manuscript.

To Barbara Tyler, former Curator of the Cole County Historical Society, who gave unstintingly of her time to locate records of this period from the society's library.

Grateful acknowledgment is also made to the following for information provided: to Joseph R. Kroeger, Sr., for his assistance in identifying local landmarks related to the Civil War period; to Mrs. John Deeken for information on the Wallendorf farm, where General Price spent his night in Jefferson City; to George and Ruth Wallendorf for their family photographs and stories of the Wallendorf farm; to Dale Turner for the 1859 drawing of Jefferson City; to Bill Fannin of the Missouri State Museum of the Department of Natural Resources for his insight and knowledge of the Civil War in Missouri; to James Joplin for providing some of the photographs of the period; to Rose Mary Moerschel Vogel and Edith Vogel for sharing documents of family legends about the Dulle home; and to Richard Terry for information on Civil War artifacts found in and around Jefferson City.

To the Chicago Historical Society for the photo of James Mulligan; and Jefferson City's Thomas Jefferson Library for the use of their excellent resource section.

To the *Columbia Missourian* for information on the Centralia Raid. To the staff of Summers Publishing: to Terri Boyce for researching and gathering the photographs; to LuAnn Frevert for editing, researching and writing portions of the text; and to John Robinson for editing and technical assistance.

Lastly, to my wife, Theresa, for patiently reading the many drafts and proofs and for correcting my many spelling errors.

Prologue

The passing decades have mantled the Civil War in romance and glamour, but it was a critical and traumatic period pitting brother against brother and neighbor against neighbor.

Jefferson City was a divided city, often a scene of chaos and confusion. Protagonists on both sides held firm to their beliefs and were ready to offer their lives for the principles they held dear. (Yet, as was demonstrated on many battlefields, they did not always lose their compassion for each other.)

Prior to the start of the Civil War, the majority of the population in the city espoused the cause of the South. There was a sound reason for this since many of the ancestors of the earliest migrants to Jefferson City could be traced to Virginia, Kentucky, Tennessee and other southern states. Family ties, the intricate web of marriages and intermarriages, loyalties to the various "home" states, and the prejudices and passions engendered by the issue of slavery drew these people into a tight knot of support for the South.

Missouri's Governor Claiborne F. Jackson, Lieutenant Governor Thomas C. Reynolds, and the General Assembly favored alignment with the South. In his inaugural address on December 31, 1860, Governor Jackson urged that Missouri would "best consult her own interests and the interests of the whole country by a timely declaration to stand by her sister slave owning states, in whose wrong she participated and with those institutions and people she sympathized." Jackson's speech was received with prolonged applause. While Jackson hoped that the North and South could reach some agreement and thereby preserve the Union, he was covertly seeking ways to lead his state into the Confederacy. He realized that the State Militia was a key to such an effort, and promptly recommended a reorganization along Confederate lines with Confederate sympathizers in command.

However, Governor Jackson's plans for secession failed, and Missourians voted at a state convention to remain in the Union.

Chronology

1861

February 28

State convention to determine relationship between Missouri and U.S. governments

March 4

Vote against secession

April 12

Following the bombardment of Fort Sumter, President Lincoln requests troops. Governor Jackson refuses; Francis Blair and Nathaniel Lyon comply

May 10

Camp Jackson seized by Lyon and Blair

May 21

Price-Harney Agreement

May 25

Sterling Price appointed Commander-in-Chief of State Militia

May 30

General Harney replaced by General Lyon

June 11

Planters' House meeting; Price and Jackson flee back to Jefferson City

June 13

Jackson leaves Jefferson City for Boonville with state records; Lyon and Blair leave St. Louis for Jefferson City

June 15
Lyon and Blair arrive in Jefferson City

June 17
Battle of Boonville; Confederates retreat south

June 30
Hamilton R. Gamble elected Governor of Missouri at state convention

July 13
Lyon moves south and arrives in Springfield

August 10
Battle of Wilson's Creek (near Springfield)

August 21
Grant reports to Jefferson City - stays one week; bushwhackers rampant

August 25
Price heads north again

September 21
Mulligan surrenders to Price at the Battle of Lexington

September 26
Fremont arrives in Jefferson City, establishes Camp Lillie and starts fortifications in anticipation that Price will attack Jefferson City

September 30
Price heads for southwest Missouri, not Jefferson City

November 2
Fremont replaced by General David Hunter

November 28

Jackson's Missouri government-in-exile admitted into the Confederacy

1862

No major military action in central Missouri; bushwhackers pillage, burn and murder

December 6

Governor Jackson (governor-in-exile) dies

1863

January 1

President Lincoln issues the Emancipation Proclamation

February 14

Thomas C. Reynolds becomes the new governor-in-exile

August 21

Order No. 11

September 22

General Joe Shelby heads toward Jefferson City

October 10

Shelby strikes Tipton, proceeds to Boonville, retreats south at Marshall

1864

September 23
Price with Shelby, Marmaduke and Fagan enter southeast Missouri with 12,000 troops

September 27
Battle of Pilot Knob

September 27
Centralia Massacre

October 7
Price moves on Jefferson City

October 8
Price leaves Jefferson City unmolested; Pleasonton arrives

October 11
Price meets with "Bloody Bill" Anderson

October 14-17
Nearly all Union troops called have reported to Jefferson City

October 23
Battle of Westport; Price flees south to Arkansas

1865

January 6
Slavery abolished at constitutional convention in St. Louis

April 9
General Lee surrenders to General Grant at Appomattox, Virginia

Part I

Background

(Dale Turner)

The first Pacific Railroad train steamed into Jefferson City in 1856. Forty years after the sparsely inhabited site on the Missouri River became the state's capital, the population had reached 3,082. This view was sketched from the vicinity of Bolivar and West Main, looking east over "Mill Bottom."

Jefferson City

Missouri's Capital

On December 31, 1821, the General Assembly of Missouri passed an act establishing the location for a permanent capital. Rivers were the major source of transportion during this era. Because the junction of the Osage and Missouri Rivers was near the middle of the state, and because the St. Louis delegation (who wanted the government to remain in the St. Louis area) was outnumbered by the combined votes of the out-state delegates, the law designated that the location of the capital be on the banks of the Missouri within 40 miles of the Osage River.

On January 11, 1822, the legislature agreed to name their capital city the "City of Jefferson." However, through common usage, it has become known as Jefferson City.

The first Missouri State Capitol Building erected in Jefferson City during 1825-1826 was on the site of the present Governor's Mansion, and the legislature met for the first time in Jefferson City in 1826. This building was destroyed by fire in 1837. A second Capitol, built near the location of the present Capitol, was completed in 1840. This was the Capitol that was considered the prize by the opposing forces of the Civil War.

By 1860 the population of Jefferson City had reached 3,082. It was a town mainly associated with the state government. The Capitol with the attendant state offices and the Governor's Mansion were located in the city.

The legislators from St. Louis and Kansas City detested Jefferson City and complained about its provincialism and the rutted streets that became quagmires of mud when it rained. Hogs wallowed in the muddy, low-lying areas and cows meandered unattended throughout the city. The legislators also complained about the lack of social life and the lack of adequate accommodations to which they were accustomed in the larger cities.

In 1860, the population in the state penitentiary in Jefferson City was nearing 500. H. Clay Ewing was mayor, the *Examiner* and the *Inquirer* were city newspapers, and the Bank of the State of Missouri had a branch facility in town. Westbound travelers transferred from the Pacific Railroad to river packet lines, and stage coach lines connected with Columbia, Fulton and Tuscumbia.

High Street, the principal street, contained the main business district and a number of hotels. (There are indications that several of the hotels along High Street were of the "sporting" variety.) Each morning wagons loaded with fresh produce from the surrounding farms parked diagonal to the curb on High Street. Matrons bargained with the peddlers or huddled in groups and exchanged gossip. Other wagons loaded with coal, wood and kerosene were parked on Madison and Monroe Streets.

The Missouri River was a vital artery to the west, and the port facilities of Jefferson City were important not only for receiving materials from St. Louis for transshipment and land transport west, but also as a port for shipment of agricultural products to St. Louis.

One of the principal shipments from Jefferson City was hides to the developing leather and shoe industry in St. Louis. Sketches of the period show that port facilities included piers and a central wharf located near the railroad station. The central wharf, in addition to handling passenger traffic, probably also served for the transfer of cargo from rail to steamers for transshipment west.

The County Seat

Jefferson City has been the seat of Cole County since January 21, 1829, when it was moved from Marion.

In 1860, of the 8,724 residents in Cole County, 167 owned 779 slaves. This compared to Missouri's population of 1,201,909, including 115,617 slaves. These slaves worked on farms, in the homes as domestics, and in one of the principal industries of Cole County — the logging and milling of the abundant ancient trees. Ties and cut lumber were required for the construction of the bridges and trestles of the Pacific Railroad (later the Missouri Pacific and now the Union Pacific System) which had reached Tipton in 1858. (From Tipton one could take the Butterfield Overland Stage all the way to San Francisco.)

There were a number of mines in the vicinity of Jefferson City. Coal was mined from slope mines south of the city. Lead mines in the Russellville area bore picturesque names such as Eureka,

Pioneer, Boaz, Guyon and Henderson. Some of these mines had attendant smelters.

The Germans

The majority of Germans who settled in and around Jefferson City were patriotic to the Union. They tolerated no sympathies with the South, and made no effort to conceal it. For deeply ingrained religious and political reasons, they were repulsed by the mere thought of servitude. Many had worked on the estates of the titled and rich in Germany and wanted no part of the life they had left behind. German migration to Missouri was encouraged by Gottfried Duden, a German living in Warren County, Missouri, who wrote a book entitled, *A Report of a Journey to the Western States of North America.* The book was widely circulated in Germany. It contained glowing accounts of the Missouri River Valley with "ground so black with humus that it seems one is walking on beds of coal." Those who were farmers in the Old Country settled in the fertile agricultural lowlands around Jefferson City for two reasons: The land in the valley of the Missouri River was rich and fertile, and being frugal, they knew a bargain when they saw one. This land could be purchased from the federal government for $1.25 to $1.50 an acre, as compared to $15 to $40 an acre in eastern states such as Maryland and Virginia.

The German artisans settled in the southwest section of Jefferson City known facetiously as Muenichberg (also spelled Munichburg) or Germantown. They established their own shops, banks, lodges and churches, and the German language was spoken almost exclusively in the shops and on the streets.

This flood into Missouri of German immigrants, many who were refugees from the unsuccessful revolutions of 1830 and 1848, threatened almost overnight to eclipse the power and influence of the entrenched "first" families who, for the most part, were Southern sympathizers. These families were clannish, suspicious and mistrustful of foreigners and aliens, and vented their suspicions on the Germans. The scornful name "Dutch" was attached to all Germans, especially in St. Louis which, at the time, was considered to be the largest "foreign" city in the United States. The Germans, free of aristocratic pretensions, looked with disdain upon the essentially Anglo snobbishness. In spite of the taunts and jibes, the Germans began to form their own militia units and secretly drilled with old German, Belgian and Austrian muskets. They were not popular among the Southern sympathizers and were subjected to devastating ridicule as being stubborn and stingy. They were portrayed with spiked mustaches, gap-toothed grins and Prussian close-cropped hair, and looked upon with shame and disgrace. They were referred to as "Lincoln Hirelings" and "Lop-eared Dutch." The most humiliating term applied to the Germans was "Hessians," a reference to the German mercenaries hired by the British to fight against the American revolutionaries. As the war progressed,

Southern sympathizers imputed a hun-like image to all German units of the Union army and warned that they would engage in murder, rape, treachery and arson.

The Germans, for their part, exemplified devotion to public service, obedience to duty, and honor in serving. Totally unselfish and incorruptible, they regarded military service as not only a patriotic duty but one to be performed modestly and completed honorably. President Lincoln later singled out German and Hungarian units as selfless and unseeking in their heroism, loyalty and courage.

A State Divided

Presidential Candidates & Platforms – 1860			
Republican	**Democrat**		
Anti-Slavery	**Conditional Slavery**		**Pro-Slavery**
Abraham Lincoln	**John C. Bell**	**Stephan A. Douglas**	**John C. Breckenridge**
Slavery should be abolished.	Union preserved in spite of the slavery issue.	Local voters given option for slavery.	Slavery should extend to the territories and be protected by the federal government.

Election of 1860

During the presidential election of 1860 the national parties were in chaotic condition. There were four candidates and four platforms on the slavery question. Stephan A. Douglas wanted the settlers of a territory to decide the issue for themselves. John C. Bell advocated that the country should remain united in spite of the slavery issue. John C. Breckenridge believed slavery should be extended into the territories and protected by the federal government. And Abraham Lincoln wanted slavery abolished.

Douglas won in Missouri, followed by Bell, Breckenridge and Lincoln. Missouri had renounced the extreme doctrines on slavery, both northern and southern, and cast her vote for a conservative policy.

The election of Claiborne F. Jackson as Missouri's governor was due in large part to his endorsement of Stephan A. Douglas. Although Jackson favored the Breckenridge ideals of secession, he sensed Douglas would win. He was right. Missouri was the only state that Douglas carried.

(State Historical Society of Missouri)

CLAIBORNE FOX JACKSON (1806-1862) from Fayette, Howard County, was elected governor in 1860. He urged the citizens of Missouri to "stand by her sister slave-holding states."

Secession?

The election of Abraham Lincoln to the Presidency in November 1860 precipitated the almost immediate secession of South Carolina from the Union. Before Lincoln could be inaugurated, six other states followed South Carolina out of the Union. Secessionist fever swept Missouri.

The Missouri legislature was hopelessly divided. The Breckenridge Democrats were more numerous, but were outnumbered by the combined vote of the Douglas and Bell factions, and the Republicans were few but active. On January 16, 1861, by a Senate vote of 31 to 2, the legislature passed a bill that allowed the citizens of Missouri to elect delegates to a state convention. In the election of these delegates, secession was presented to the people as a political issue for the first time.

The result of the February 18 election was a surprise to all and a disappointment to the extreme Southern sympathizers. Of the ninety-nine delegates (3 delegates from each senatorial district), not a single advocate of secession was elected. The people had spoken, not so much against secession or that the majority were uncompromisingly Union, but rather for a delay and compromise for the preservation of the Union.

On February 28, 1861, the state convention met in Jefferson City to consider a draft resolution on the proposed relationship between the state government and the government of the United States. Because of his natural leadership ability and his tremendous

(State Historical Society of Missouri)

STERLING PRICE (1809-1867) was Missouri's governor from 1853 to 1857. Although a member of the Conditional Union Party of Missouri, he sympathized with the Southern cause and joined their ranks in 1861, when Governor Jackson appointed him major general of the State Militia.

personal popularity, Sterling Price was elected chairman of the convention. "Old Pap" Price was a former Governor of Missouri, a distinguished veteran of the Mexican War, and although he was a slave owner, he was a Conditional Union man.

Without delay, the decision was made "to remove its sessions from the hostile atmosphere of Jefferson City [pro-Southern] to the more congenial air of St. Louis [pro-Northern]," but not before the convention was addressed by a German native of Austria, Isador Bush, of St. Louis. He declared almost prophetically:

> While you, Mr. President, and all members of this convention, I believe, only imagine the horrors of war, and fancy the evils of revolution, I know them. My eyes have seen what you cannot imagine, what I cannot describe — the terrors of civil war, of bloodshed and revolution. Yet should a conflict be inevitable, I pledge myself that your German fellow-citizens will stand by the Government and the Union. They love peace but the history of their own thirty-four confederated states of distracted Germany teaches them there is no peace and no liberty without union.

On March 4, 1861, Lincoln took the oath of office in Washington, D.C., and on the same day, the state convention that convened in the Mercantile Liberty Hall in St. Louis voted against secession. Although it agreed to reconvene in Jefferson City on July 22, 1861, events leading to war soon overtook the proposed convention.

The bombardment of Ft. Sumter on April 12, 1861, produced a ponderously solemn air in Jefferson City. The fever of the approaching conflict was sweeping the city, splitting groups, friends and families. On April 15, Lincoln issued a proclamation requiring that an army of 75,000 troops be raised, and that each state contribute its share. Missouri was asked to furnish four infantry regiments. The thought had been expressed by many Unionists that Governor Jackson was intriguing with the Confederacy to deliver the state into the secessionist ranks. Their fears were justified when Governor Jackson responded defiantly to Lincoln: "There can be, I apprehend, no doubt that these men are intended to form a part of the President's army to make war upon the people of the seceded states. Your requisition, in my judgment, is illegal, unconstitutional, and revolutionary in its objects, inhuman and diabolical and cannot be complied with. Not a man will the State of Missouri furnish to carry out such an unholy crusade."

Union Leaders and the Home Guard

Jackson's opposition was centered in St. Louis, with Francis (Frank) P. Blair, Jr., the leader of the Unionists. Blair, a 40-year-old Kentuckian, had come to Missouri in 1843 to study law in the offices of his brother, Judge Montgomery Blair, who later was Lincoln's Postmaster General. Frank Blair was elected to Congress in 1856 and 1860, but resigned his seat in 1862. He was not only opposed to slavery, having freed his slaves in 1859, but was also bitterly opposed to secession. He vowed to fight to keep Missouri in the Union. Blair formed the Wide Awakes to protect speakers at political gatherings. They later became the basis for the pro-Union Home Guard. Because of his fearless courage and speaking ability, he was recognized as the leader of the Unconditional Union Men of Missouri.

Blair countered Jackson's refusal to Lincoln by promptly raising from the St. Louis area four Federal regiments of three-month enlistees. He selected a Union firebrand, Captain Nathaniel Lyon, as his military advisor. Possessed of tireless energy and intense conviction, Lyon exuded the impatience and lack of self-control which characterized the widespread intolerance for those sympathizing with the Confederates.

(State Historical Society of Missouri)

FRANCIS P. BLAIR, JR. (1821-1875) was a powerful force in Missouri politics for many years. He sided with the North during the Civil War, and by 1865, held the rank of major general in the Union Army.

(State Historical Society of Missouri)

NATHANIEL LYON (1818-1861), an ardent opponent of slavery, was commissioned a brigadier general in 1861, and assigned the command of the Department of the West.

(James Joplin)

FRANCES CLALIN (alias ALBERT CASHIER) fought for the Union, purportedly with the 4th Mo. Heavy Artillery and 13 Mo. Cavalry, Co. A. Recruitment procedures were inadequate, to say the least, and the fact she was a female went undetected until 1911 following an automobile accident. She continued to draw a pension until her death in 1915.

Confederate Leaders and the State Militia

Governor Jackson called for advice from Sterling Price. Although former Governor Price favored the Conditional Union position, he was also a plantation owner and his sympathies ultimately leaned toward the South.

Born in Virginia, Price came to Missouri in 1831. After living in Fayette for two years, he moved to Chariton County where he engaged in farming and mercantile business. As a young man of 22, Price embarked on a remarkable political career, serving as a member of the state legislature, later as its Speaker, and then as a Missouri congressman. His career culminated in 1852 when he was elected Governor of Missouri. Commissioned by President Polk, Price fought in the 1846 to 1848 Mexican Campaign, and was respected throughout Missouri not only for his political astuteness but for his military abilities.

One of Price's principal lieutenants was a young, handsome, and dashing 6-footer named John Sappington Marmaduke. He had a great mane of warrior hair and a full, soft beard. Unmarried, John Marmaduke was sought after by the ladies of the first families of Missouri. His father, M. M. Marmaduke, was a governor of Missouri and Governor Claiborne Jackson was his uncle. Educated at Yale, Harvard and West Point, he was a consummate horseman and skilled marksman. At sunrise on September 6, 1863, General Marmaduke fought a duel with fellow General Lucius M. Walker. General Walker fell mortally wounded and died the following day.

(State Historical Society of Missouri)

JOHN SAPPINGTON MARMADUKE (1833-1887) sided with his uncle, Governor Claiborne Jackson, and joined the Confederate forces as a colonel in 1861. By 1865 he had obtained the rank of major general. In 1884 he was elected Governor of Missouri, a position his father, M. M. Marmaduke, had also held.

The pro-Southern State Militia was in desperate need of supplies and arms. Governor Jackson had previously surveyed the available arms in the Jefferson City Armory, a multi-storied building located on the southwest corner of the Capitol grounds, across the street from St. Peter's Church. There were seven artillery pieces that had been used in either the War of 1812 or the Mexican Campaign. There were also a few hundred flintlock muskets. The seven cannon had been sent to the St. Louis Armory to be recast and caissons and carriages made for them. A cartridge factory had been established at the penitentiary. Some of the muskets were converted into percussion weapons and a few of the muskets were rifled.

(Dr. Joseph S. Summers, Jr

If the pro-Southern forces could be adequately equipped, it was reasoned that they would be able to consolidate their gains and press home their advantage to bring Missouri into the Confederacy. Governor Jackson began to mobilize the State Militia under pro-Southern officers. A number of Confederate-sympathizing troops suddenly appeared in Jefferson City. The State Militia consisted of nine divisions (one for each Congressional district) and at its greatest strength totaled 11,000 men. A clipping from the May 25, 1861, Jefferson City *Examiner* states that former Governor Sterling Price was appointed Commander-in-Chief of the State Militia. Also appointed were Adjutant General Warwick Hough and Quartermaster General James S. Harding.

OPPOSITE: At the time the Civil War broke out, the Armory in Jefferson City held few munitions. Built in 1860 and located on the Capitol grounds, the Armory held a total inventory of seven artillery pieces dating back to the War of 1812 and the Mexican Campaign and a few hundred flintlock muskets.

Camp Jackson

On April 20, 1861, about 200 Southern sympathizers seized the U.S. Arsenal at Liberty, Missouri. Jackson, however, had a bigger prize in mind — the U.S. Arsenal at St. Louis with its 60,000 muskets, ammunition and artillery. Envoys were dispatched to Jefferson Davis for sufficient artillery and ammunition to capture the arsenal. Davis responded with a large amount of war materiel, disguised

JEFFERSON DAVIS (1808-1889) was inaugurated as the President of the Confederate States of America on February 18, 1861. He led the Southern cause until his capture in Georgia on May 10, 1865. In 1867 he was allowed to go to Canada. Twice indicted for treason, the proceedings were dropped after the general amnesty proclamation of December 25, 1868.

(State Historical Society of Missouri)

(State Historical Society of Missouri)

The St. Louis Arsenal was a storehouse for 60,000 guns and ammunition which the Confederates desperately needed to equip their army.

as commodities such as marble and ale, and shipped to St. Louis on a steamboat. Arriving at St. Louis, the materiel was promptly transferred to Camp Jackson, where the State Militia, composed primarily of Southern sympathizers, was drilling. Alarmed, Lyon and Blair formed a fighting group of some 7,000 troops, many of them German, and on May 10 marched on and captured the camp and supplies.

When Lyon began to march prisoners out of camp, a crowd of Southern sympathizers started a hostile demonstration against

Lyon's men, especially the German units like Die Schwarze Garde (The Black Guard). They shouted vulgar epithets, and hurled rocks, brickbats and other missiles at the troops. A full riot ensued. When it was over, fifteen persons had been killed and scores wounded.

News of the capture of Camp Jackson was received in Jefferson City between five and six o'clock on May 10, and produced a great panic in the legislature, which was in session. George Graham Vest leaped onto a chair and waved a dispatch before the assembly shouting, "Frank Blair, Captain Lyon and the Dutch have seized Camp Jackson." The military bill conscripting all able-bodied men into the State Militia (which was pending in the House) was passed within fifteen minutes.

Shortly after midnight the whole town was awakened by the ringing of bells and the shouts of men calling the members of the legislature. A dispatch had been received that 2,000 Federal troops had left St. Louis at 11:00 o'clock to capture the governor, the legislature and the state officers. The rumor proved groundless.

The next day the true state of affairs became known. The total number of prisoners captured at Camp Jackson and taken to the St. Louis Arsenal was 50 officers and 639 privates. Lyon and Blair had arranged for the removal and transfer of all muskets (except for some which Blair used to arm his own men) from the St. Louis Arsenal to Illinois.

Part II

War 1861

Negotiations Fail

Price-Harney Agreement

Although Governor Jackson made some conciliatory overtures to keep Missouri out of the War, General Lyon continued to press Blair to display a greater militancy toward the governor. General W.S. Harney, the U.S. Military Commander in St. Louis, while proclaiming that full Federal power would be exerted to keep Missouri in the Union, had no desire to engage in war unless forced to do so. He notified General Price to meet him in St. Louis. On May 21, 1861, they came to an understanding which became known as *The Price-Harney Agreement*. Jackson felt that a way for reestablishment of harmonious relations had been opened by the agreement. However, there was great dissatisfaction among the Unionists concerning the agreement, and General Lyon and Frank Blair conspired and complained to President Lincoln to have General Harney removed. Harney was removed on May 30, 1861, and Lyon was put in command of St. Louis and Missouri and all territory between the Mississippi River and the Rockies, except Texas, New Mexico and Utah.

The Price Harney Agreement

St. Louis, May 21, 1861

The undersigned, officers of the United States government and of the government of the State of Missouri, for the purpose of removing misapprehensions and allaying public excitement, deem it proper to declare publicly that they have this day had a personal interview in this city, in which it has been mutually understood, without the semblance of dissent on either part, that each of them has no other than a common object equally interesting and important to every citizen of Missouri – that of restoring peace and good order to the people of that state in subordination to the laws of the general and state governments. It being thus understood, there seems no reason why every citizen should not confide in the proper officers of the general and state governments to restore quiet, and, as among the best means of offering no counter-influences, we mutually recommend to all persons to respect each other's rights throughout the state, making no attempt to exercise unauthorized powers, as it is the determination of the proper authorities to suppress all unlawful proceedings, which can only disturb the public peace.

General Price, having by commission full authority over the militia of the State of Missouri, undertakes, with the sanction of the governor the state already declared, to direct the whole power of the state officers to maintain order within the state among the people thereof, and General Harney publicly declares that, this object being thus assured, he can have no other occasion, as he has no wish, to make military movements, which might otherwise create excitements and jealosies which he most earnestly desires to avoid.

We, the undersigned, do mutually enjoin upon the people of the state to attend to their civil business of whatever sort it may be, and it is hoped that the unquiet elements which have threatened so seriously to disturb public peace may soon subside and be remembered only to be deplored.

Sterling Price
Major-General Missouri State Guard
William S. Harney
Brigadier-General Commanding

(State Historical Society of Missouri)

WILLIAM SELBY HARNEY (1800-1889), a Union general and Commander of the Department of the West in St. Louis, met with General Sterling Price in that city on May 21, 1861, and agreed "to make no military movements" in the state. The agreement, however, was short-lived. General Harney was relieved of his St. Louis command shortly thereafter.

Planters' House Meeting

General Price and Governor Jackson immediately sought an audience with the new Union general. On June 11, 1861, accompanied by the governor's aide, Thomas L. Snead, they arrived in St. Louis by special train. They proceeded to the Planters' House for a meeting with General Lyon, Colonel Frank Blair and Major H. A. Conant which lasted four hours. The meeting failed to produce an agreement, and General Lyon abruptly ended the session saying, "This means war. In one hour one of my officers will call for you and conduct you out of my lines." Without another word, he stormed out of the room with spurs rattling and saber clanking. The search for peaceful solutions had been abandoned — reason, tolerance and compromise were rejected for armed violence.

OPPOSITE: At the Planters' House meeting in St. Louis, General Lyon, Francis Blair, Claiborne Jackson and General Price, along with their aides (not pictured) Thomas L. Snead and Major H. A. Conant, tried one last time to negotiate an agreement between the pro-Union and the pro-Confederate factions.

(State Historical Society of Missouri)

Strategies Planned

Jackson Leaves and Takes Seal and State Records

Without hesitation, Price and Jackson left the Planters' House, returned to the train and rushed back to Jefferson City. To hinder any possible Union advance by rail, Price ordered the burning of the bridges over the Gasconade and Osage Rivers. They arrived in Jefferson City at 2:00 on the morning of June 12, 1861, and convened a meeting with House and Senate leaders explaining that there was no doubt in their minds that General Lyon would soon be attacking Jefferson City. As clerks were told to pack all state documents for transport, with the idea that an alternate capital would be established elsewhere in the state, panic ensued in the various state offices.

A crossroads between North and South, and the Union East and undetermined West, Missouri held the gateway for invasion by either side during the Civil War. Governor Jackson and General Price called up the State Militia for service on the Southern side, knowing that General Lyon and Colonel Blair would quickly assume the Federal offensive. On June 12, 1861, Jackson called for 50,000 volunteers to defend the state. Rebel sympathizers of all descriptions descended on Jefferson City by coach, rail, steamer, wagon and horseback, but in far less numbers than called by the governor. Most of the recruits were poorly armed and many were without weapons of any kind. Few had any military training, and practically all were totally unprepared for organized combat.

On June 13, Governor Jackson, General Price, and several state officials left for Boonville with the Missouri State Seal and many of the state's records. That same day, General Lyon and Frank Blair left St. Louis for Jefferson City with approximately 2,000 men on the river steamers *Iatan*, *McDowell*, *Louisiana* and *Swan*.

Samuel L. Clemens and the Ralls County Rangers

(State Historical Society of Missouri)

With the principal railroad bridges burned, the Federals needed competent river pilots to transport troops by steamboat for an attack on Jefferson City. It so happened that a young river pilot and Southern sympathizer was in St. Louis to renew his pilot's license. He was asked to pilot one of the Federal river packets. Explaining that he was a Mississippi River pilot, not a Missouri River pilot, he was asked to stand by in case he was needed. In the confusion of finding steamboats and loading the troops and supplies, the young pilot, Samuel Langhorne Clemens, managed to leave unnoticed and return to his home city of Hannibal.

Back in Hannibal, Clemens joined the Ralls County Rangers, a Confederate group organized to defend their county against "the Dutch." Every man furnished his own mount and weapon and, while most farm boys were mounted on trim horseflesh, Clemens rode into camp on a yellow mule. Armed with a squirrel rifle, he looked more like one of the humorous characters in his books than the imposing soldier he imagined himself. When word of the formation of the Rangers reached General Lyon, he sent a column of the Twenty-first Illinois stationed at Mexico, Missouri, under the command of Colonel Ulysses S. Grant, to seek out the unit. The Rangers were bivouacked in a hayloft when a careless smoker's pipe set the hay aflame. In the exodus, Sam Clemens jumped ungracefully from the loft and sprained his ankle. Realizing that war was not the grand adventure he surmised, as soon as his ankle healed, Clemens set off for Carson City, Nevada, where his brother was the newly-appointed territorial secretary.

Grant and Clemens met again in later years under entirely different circumstances. Clemens (Mark Twain) became a close friend of Grant. Grant, heavily in debt and suffering from cancer, was encouraged by Twain to write his memoirs. Twain arranged for the publication of the memoirs, which earned Grant a half million dollars. Today, the two volumes are hailed as being among the best memoirs ever written.

Lyon and Blair Take Control of Jefferson City

On June 15, 1861, General Lyon and Frank Blair disembarked from the *Iatan* at Jefferson City where a large crowd of Union sympathizers gathered on a levee near the penitentiary to greet them. Colonel Thomas L. Price, a prominent Unionist and no relative of General Price, was the first to greet General Lyon and Frank Blair. (Colonel Price lived in a mansion where the Supreme Court now stands.) The German population of Jefferson City warmly welcomed the Union troops, many of whom were of German descent. Several soldiers ascended the cupola of the Capitol and displayed the American flag. Others fanned out through the city looking for residences displaying Confederate flags and arrested known Southern sympathizers. Prisoners were taken to a dungeon created in the basement of the Capitol. The prisoners, including the son of the governor, were sketched by an artist from *Harper's Weekly*. Although there was passive acceptance of the Union troops, many Southern sympathizers resented the many troops who spoke with a decided German accent.

OPPOSITE: This *Harper's Weekly* sketch of October 5, 1861, shows rebel prisoners in the dungeon of the State Capitol Building in Jefferson City. The man wearing the hat and standing behind the barrel was the son of Governor Claiborne Jackson.

U.S. volunteers under General Lyon disembarked on June 15, 1861, near the penitentiary in Jefferson City. The *Iatan* has been immortalized in the official seal of the City of Jefferson.

North and South Meet on Missouri Soil

Battle of Boonville

Learning that General Price, Governor Jackson and their command had left Jefferson City for Boonville two days before, General Lyon took off in pursuit, leaving Colonel Henry Boernstein in command of three companies (about 300 men). The weather was unbearably hot and Colonel Boernstein encamped his troops in the cool assembly chambers of the state Capitol where they stacked their arms and knapsacks along the corridors. Colonel Boernstein, a trained Austrian soldier, university graduate, and editor of the powerful *Anzeiger des Westens* in St. Louis, got along famously with the Germans in Jefferson City.

General Lyon caught up with Jackson's forces on June 17, 1861, at Boonville. Although referred to as the Battle of Boonville, it was, in reality, a brief skirmish that lasted twenty minutes in which the superiority of Union troops prevailed and the Pro-Southern forces were routed and driven from the field of battle. Lyon did not pursue the retreating forces and they moved unmolested to southern Missouri. This defeat made it impossible for Missouri to secede from the Union at that time.

Union sympathizers in Jefferson City burst with excitement over the news of the Union victory at Boonville and young men gathered at the recruiting stations to enlist in the Union army. Confident that their foes would run at the first shot, the

(State Historical Society of Missouri)

The Battle of Boonville was the first hostile field engagement in Missouri. Although the fighting was short-lived and the casualties were few, the Union victory on June 17, 1861, was a blow to the volunteer forces of Governor Jackson, and seriously threatened the volunteer enlistments in Price's army.

raw recruits in their naive enthusiasm regarded war as a grand adventure. Glancing over the roster of Cole County veterans that served in the Civil War on the Union side reveals names [spellings may vary] like Eveler, Hoffmeyer, Jobe, Ihler, Kroeger, Loeschner, Ott, Opel, Prenger, Rackers, Rost, Schwaler, Schneider, Scruggs, Weckenberg, Vogel and Zimmerman. On the Confederate side are such names as Bayse, Barnd, Bragg, Clark, Duncan, Dixon, Ewing, Hale, Lay, Parsons, Matthews, Standish and Davison.

On July 27, Colonel Boernstein's regiment was ordered back to St. Louis from Jefferson City. They were replaced by Colonel James A. Mulligan and his Irish Brigade from Chicago. The Brigade, referred to as "a fine body of men and the officers are gentlemen," and approximately 900 Home Guard soldiers were quartered at the Jefferson City Fair Grounds (presently the Fairmount Court area).

MISSOURIANS!

TO ARMS!

THE NEW REGIMENT OF

Missouri Riflemen!

HAS BEEN ACCEPTED, AND WILL BE MUSTERED INTO SERVICE AT THE ARSENAL IMMEDIATELY.

☞Companies will have transportation afforded them from any point on the rivers or railroads, and will be received and cared for by an officer of the Regiment.

☞Companies wanting service, should make immediate application, as the regiment will be full in a few days.

JULY 24th, 1861.

(State Historical Society of Missour

Battle of Wilson's Creek

After the defeat at Boonville, General Price and his Missouri State Militia sought the isolation and vastness of the mountains of south Missouri to raise and train a new army. One of Price's remarkable gifts was his ability to whip armies into shape — to train farmhands and mountain boys in the rudiments of the soldier's art within a few weeks time. Price's Missouri troops were joined by General Ben McCulloch's Confederates from Arkansas.

General Lyon moved southward, arriving in Springfield on July 13. He conducted an inspection of his troops and supplies, and appealed to Maj. Gen. John C. Fremont, commander of the Western Department, for more of both. His urgent appeals were not honored.

On August 10, 1861, Union and Confederate armies clashed at Wilson's Creek, ten miles southwest of Springfield. Although displaying incredible bravery, General Lyon was killed along with 1,302 of his soldiers. Lyon's army was in a state of almost total rout, its units scattered and its forces demoralized. After Wilson's Creek, every military advantage lay with Generals Price and McCulloch. However, differences between the two men prevented Price's pursuit of the fleeing Federals, most of whom probably could have been captured before they reached Rolla, the terminus of the railroad leading to St. Louis. McCulloch had refused to cooperate until Price made an army of his "half-starved infantry and his huckleberry cavalry."

A quotation from a Jefferson City newspaper of August 10, 1911, illustrates a personal side of the conflict:

> There are four survivors in the city of the battle of Wilson's Creek, which was fought fifty years ago today near Springfield. Fred Buehrle is the lone Union survivor while Capt. J.L. Keown, Waller Bolton and Tom Schwantzott were all in the Confederate lines on that eventful day.
>
> Two of these survivors met by chance on the streets of the city this morning and exchanged recollections of the great battle, in which General Lyons attacked the Confederate forces by surprise. Fred Buehrle, almost eighty years of age and Capt. J.L. Keown, now 90 years of age were the old veterans to meet on the streets. Few citizens in this city know the thrilling experience gone through by these two veterans on that day. During the battle Fred Buehrle was struck by a bullet near the hip and fell to the ground. The Confederate forces were not far distant and among them was Capt. J.L. Keown. He saw Buehrle fall and within a short time was at his side with a quantity of water sufficient to quench the thirst of the man in opposite ranks. He stayed with him as long as he could and hurried back to the Confederate ranks.

OPPOSITE: On August 10, 1861, the combined Southern army of nearly 11,000 troops met Lyon's forces estimated between 5,000 and 6,000 soldiers at the Battle of Wilson's Creek, ten miles south of Springfield. Following the Confederate victory, McCulloch refused to join Price in pursuing the disorganized Union army.

(State Historical Society of Missouri)

BEN McCULLOCH (1811-1862), a former Texas Ranger, marched his Arkansas troops into Missouri to reinforce Price at Wilson's Creek. General McCulloch, appalled at the undisciplined, poorly-equipped Missouri troops, refused to collaborate unless he was given the chief command.

(State Historical Society of Missouri)

(State Historical Society of Missouri)

(State Historical Society of Missouri)

Early in the engagement at Wilson's Creek, General Nathaniel Lyon suffered wounds in the leg and in the head. Limping from the leg wound and with blood running down his cheek, he was determined to show his troops they still had a leader. Remounted on an orderly's horse, General Lyon had traveled only a few yards when he was fatally shot.

Two Missouri Governments

A New Governor for Missouri

With the departure of Governor Jackson and other state officials, along with the state records, all civil administration abruptly ceased. To remedy the situation, a committee of the state convention charged with the duty of reconvening the assembly met on July 6, 1861. They called upon the state convention to meet in Jefferson City on July 22.

A committee of seven was then appointed to consider several resolutions relative to problems facing the state. They presented their report to the assembly on July 25.

On July 30, 1861, the members of the state convention declared all state offices to be vacant and the next day elected Hamilton R. Gamble as governor and Willard P. Hall, lieutenant governor.

OPPOSITE: HAMILTON R. GAMBLE (1798-1864) was elected Missouri's provisional governor on July 31, 1861, forty-eight days after Governor Claiborne Jackson's hasty departure from Jefferson City. Gamble, a St. Louis attorney, was a conservative Union supporter.

(State Historical Society of Missouri)

Jackson's Missouri Government-in-Exile

In August of 1861, Governor Jackson still considered himself the rightful governor of the state and, on August 5, he proclaimed Missouri a free republic.

On October 21, a meeting of his legislature, composed of Southern sympathizers, met 200 miles southwest of Jefferson City in Neosho, Missouri. The assembly consisted of 23 senators and 77 representatives. Although it is quite probable neither house had a quorum present, an ordinance of secession was passed, and the Constitution of the Confederate States of America was ratified.

Feeling increased pressure from advancing Federals, the assembly moved several miles southeast. On October 31, they reconvened in Cassville, Missouri, where they acted on several other measures introduced by Jackson.

Jackson's Missouri was admitted into the Confederacy in November of 1861 [sources vary considerably as to the exact date].

Many Missourians sympathetic to the Southern cause had moved southward with their slaves and personal property. Governor Jackson and Lieutenant Governor Reynolds followed, carrying with them the Great Seal of the State of Missouri.

A temporary seat of government for the Confederate State of Missouri was established at Camden, Arkansas, about 75 miles south of Little Rock.

(State Historical Society of Missouri)

The Masonic Hall at Neosho, 200 miles southwest of Jefferson City, served as the first "Confederate Capitol" for Jackson's government. This building no longer exists.

Many denominations of promissory notes were issued by the government-in-exile to help finance the Confederate cause.

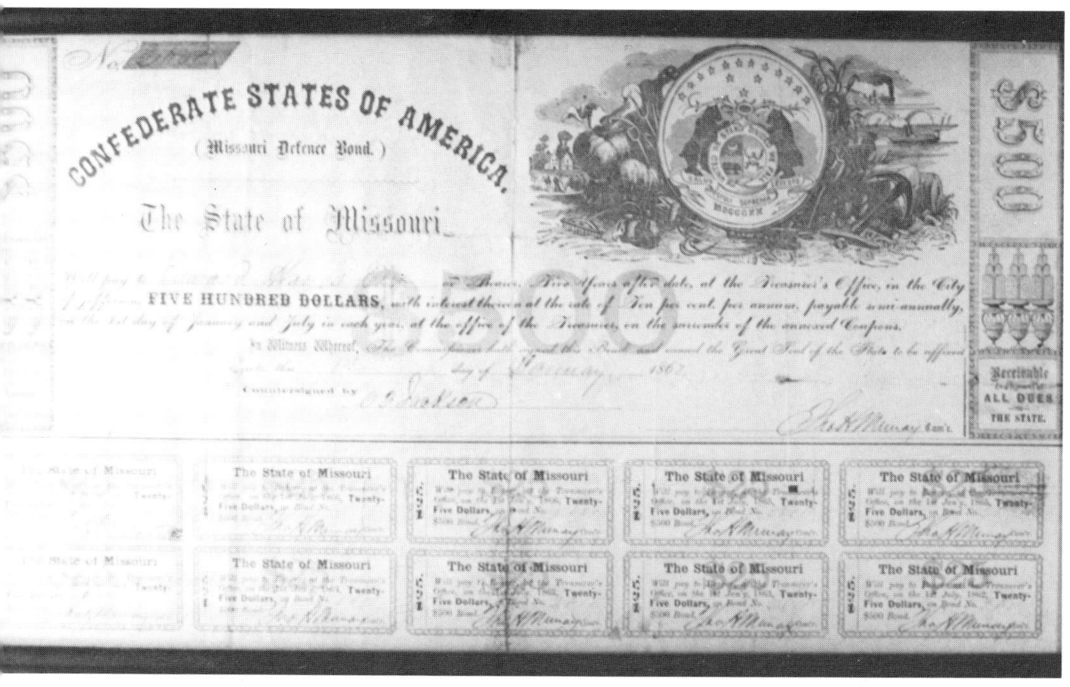

(James Joplin)

$500 debenture bonds countersigned by Governor Jackson were issued in 1862. The bearer clipped the coupon and redeemed it for $25 on the date specified. This was a Confederate bond that carried the Great Seal of the State of Missouri, which had been taken from Jefferson City.

Grant Comes To Jefferson City

Concerned that Confederate forces might attempt to take Jefferson City, Western District Commander General Fremont called upon newly-promoted Brigadier General Ulysses S. Grant who had served with the Twenty-first Illinois at Mexico, Missouri, and later at Ironton, to proceed to Jefferson City and construct a system of defenses.

Disheveled in dress, hard in drink, pungent in speech, and quick in sizing up situations and making decisions, Grant arrived in Jefferson City on August 21, 1861. He looked with disfavor on this assignment. He knew little about engineering problems concerned with defensive measures, and felt he would be more useful conducting offensive military operations against the South. In addition, Grant probably felt that the Jefferson City assignment was beneath the dignity of his newly-obtained star.

Grant found the situation in Jefferson City abominable. Although there were plenty of recruits, he found them a totally unmilitary lot, lacking in training, without arms and equipment, and bumbling in drill. Grant's initial inspection showed that the available artillery consisted of five cannons: four 6-pounders but no gunners trained to fire them, and a 24-pounder that was too cumbersome for field service. There was no artillery ammunition whatsoever, and the supply of rifle ammunition amounted to no more than 10 rounds

(James Joplin)

ULYSSES S. GRANT (1822-1885) was in Jefferson City for such a brief time, many Civil War historical accounts overlook the Jefferson City assignment. Grant was commissioned a lieutenant general in 1864 and given supreme command of all the armies of the United States. In 1869, General Grant became the 18th president of the United States.

per man.

Grant was also disturbed that there was no engineering support assigned to the Jefferson City command to help him lay out the defenses. He admitted he had forgotten most of what he had learned at West Point about the construction of defenses: He wrote, "I have no desire to gain a 'Pillow notoriety' for a branch of service that I have forgotten all about." The Pillow reference was to Confederate General Gideon Pillow, who during the Mexican Campaign had gained notoriety for his propensity to build defensive fortifications in the wrong places. Grant remembered General Pillow with distaste, and frequently expressed his contempt for him. On August 23, Grant scornfully responded to Fremont, "I am not fortifying here at all. With the picket guard and other duty coming upon the men of this command there is little time for drilling. Drill and discipline are more necessary for the men than fortification."

The recruiting methods practiced in Jefferson City incensed Grant. The law required that all recruits must serve for three years or to the end of the war. Grant described his perplexion in his *Personal Memoirs of U.S. Grant:* "In Jefferson City in August 1861, they were recruited for different periods and on different conditions; some were enlisted for six months, some for a year, some without conditions as to where they were to serve, others were not to be sent out of the state."

Bushwhackers and Refugees

In the area surrounding Jefferson City rebel marauders were driving Union sympathizers from their homes and appropriating their property, animals, hay and grain. Grant was appalled at the agitation and looked to the Home Guards in garrison at the fairgrounds with the hope that they might be organized to pursue the Confederate bands. After inspecting them, he found that some had mounts and some had weapons while others were unarmed. There was neither a post commissary nor a post quartermaster in Jefferson City, and clothing, tents and blankets were wanting. Frustrated, Grant wrote, "I have not been able to make head or tail about them, notwithstanding all my efforts."

Jefferson City was swarming with refugees — farmers, many of them Germans, who had fled the bushwhackers that operated in Cole, Boone, Osage and Callaway Counties. Inspecting the refugees, Grant found, "They were in deplorable condition and must have starved but for the support the government gave them. They had generally made their escape with a team or two, sometimes a yoke of oxen with a mule or horse in the lead. A little bedding besides their clothing and some food had been thrown in the wagon. All else of their worldly goods were abandoned and appropriated by their former neighbors." The refugees settled mainly in the western section of the city along Wears Creek, which provided water for their animals. This area was also known as Goose Bottom because of the many ducks and geese that were raised there, and skimmed along in the creek. Many of the refugee families later settled and built homes along McCarty Street. The southern and eastern portions of Jefferson City contained soldiers in garrisons and fortifications. They did not want to deal with the additional problem of refugees.

Toward the end of August, Grant wrote his father about the misery the bushwhackers were inflicting on the area surrounding Jefferson City in their efforts to gather supplies, horses and transportation for the Confederate fall campaign: "The country West of here will be left in a starving condition for the next winter. Families are being driven away in great numbers for their Union sentiments, leaving behind farms, crops and all. A sad state of affairs must exist under the most favorable circumstances that can take place. There will be no money in the Country and the entire crop will be carried off together with all stock of any value."

Meanwhile, German newspapers in Missouri were bitterly complaining that the bushwhackers were not only killing anyone who spoke with a German accent, but were now killing anyone that had a "German face."

Grant Reassigned

One week after arriving in Jefferson City Ulysses S. Grant received orders to take command of the District of Southeastern Missouri at Cape Girardeau. Shortly thereafter, he was ordered to Cairo, Illinois, and was given commands of ever-increasing responsibility which always ended in brilliant Union victories. When Lincoln was considering Grant for command of the Union Army, he was warned that Grant was a heavy drinker. Lincoln replied, "By the way, gentlemen, can either of you tell me where General Grant procures his whiskey? Because, if I can find out, I will send every General in the field a barrel of it!"

Fremont in Command

John C. Fremont, the intrepid pioneer and celebrated "Pathfinder of the West," was California's first senator and the unsuccessful Republican candidate for president in 1856. He was made a major general by Lincoln and given command of the newly-created Western Department headquartered in St. Louis. Fremont's impulsiveness and charlatanism in speech and manner of military matters caused Lincoln endless trouble. Politically astute but militarily inept, a legend had grown up about him. He had married Senator Thomas Hart Benton's daughter, Jessie, and had basked in Washington's society as a restless, seeking, perennially dissatisfied opportunist.

The Confederate victory at Bull Run, Virginia, on July 21, 1861, and the victory at Wilson's Creek, Missouri, on August 10, 1861, compounded the exhilaration of the Southerners, but had a depressing effect on the Federals. Mounting criticism was directed at Fremont, but he continued his lifestyle in St. Louis surrounded by colorfully uniformed bodyguards and glittering aides-de-camp selected without regard to their military abilities. Fremont dreamed exalted dreams about an offensive campaign that would cut deeply into the South, allowing him to seize Memphis, Little Rock and New Orleans. Fremont, however, also remained in close contact with what was happening in Washington. Major General George B.

(State Historical Society of Missouri)

JOHN CHARLES FREMONT (1830-1890), explorer of the American frontier, soldier and politician, was opposed to slavery. On July 25, 1861, he was appointed a major general by fellow-Republican President Lincoln and placed in command of the Department of the West headquartered in St. Louis.

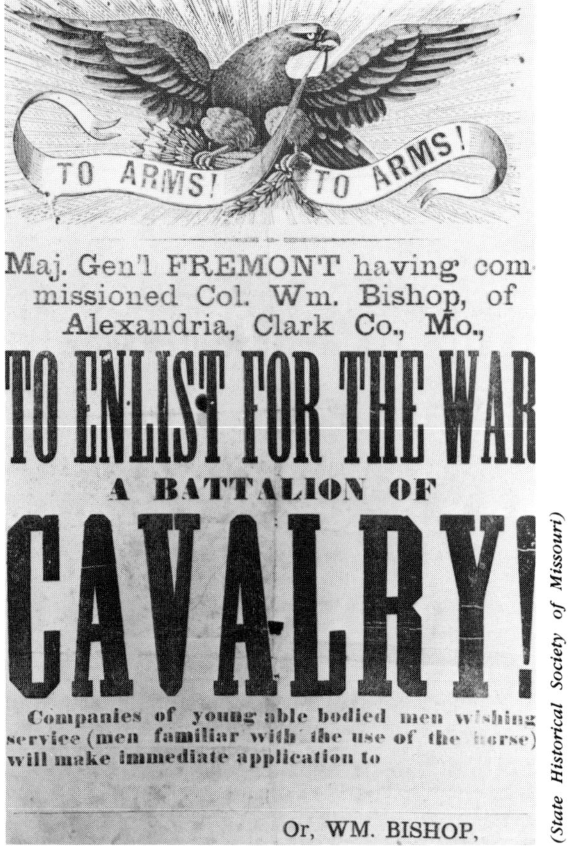

(State Historical Society of Missouri)

McClellan, who succeeded General Irvin McDowell as Commander of the Army of the Potomac, had endorsed a proposal to construct a massive defensive system of forts, lunettes, redoubts and batteries of guns situated on strategic hills encircling the city to guard all approaches to Washington.

Fremont followed suit in St. Louis and proceeded to surround the city on the north, west and south with earthworks in which he placed large-caliber guns. These guns could sweep all the roads leading to the city with grape shot and canister.

Fremont Issues Edict

The turbulence and disorder in Missouri following the Union defeat at Wilson's Creek prompted General Fremont to declare martial law throughout the state. He proclaimed that men found with arms within the line of occupation (which extended from Leavenworth, Kansas, by way of posts in Jefferson City, Rolla, Ironton, to Cape Girardeau) would be tried by court-martial and, if found guilty, would be shot. Slaves belonging to masters disloyal to the United States would be freed.

Lincoln hastily disowned and rescinded Fremont's proclamation, but not before it provoked a counterproclamation from Confederate Jeff Thompson, the ex-mayor of St. Joseph. Thompson promised that for every soldier in allegiance to the South who was put to death pursuant to Fremont's order, he would hang, draw, and quarter a Union man in retaliation.

During the winter of 1861-1862, Lincoln began advocating in the border states "compensated abolishment" (i.e., paying loyal slaveholders for their slaves and then at an appropriate time issuing a proclamation freeing the slaves in those states which were in rebellion.)

Price Victor at Lexington

Taking advantage of the large number of recruits that flocked to his standard after Wilson's Creek, General Price assembled an army and decided on August 25, 1861, to head north again. This time he took a force of about 20,000 men to break the Union patrols that had been established on the Missouri River at Boonville, Jefferson City and Kansas City.

Colonel James A. Mulligan, in Jefferson City, learned about Price's northern movement but was unaware of his destination. Perhaps, he reasoned, Price was headed for Jefferson City, and Mulligan prepared to defend the city. Mulligan, recently married, could have waited in his comfortable surroundings at the Capitol; but he was an excessively ambitious Chicago politician, and when he learned that Price was headed toward Kansas City, he and his Irish Brigade left Jefferson City in pursuit. Although the roads were quagmires of mud, Mulligan plodded along and eventually joined a Union force commanded by Colonel Thomas A. Marshall at Lexington. The two men compared commissions. Although Mulligan held seniority and was placed in charge, the two native-born commanders were in plaintive agreement about Lincoln's army of "Yer dam Dutchmen, yer Poles, Eyetalians, yer Swiss, Danes and French." Mulligan surveying the situation and seeing his forces greatly outnumbered, telegraphed Fremont that reinforcements were needed immediately. His urgent requests were not honored and the Battle of Lexington was enjoined. Mulligan was forced to surrender to Price on September 20, 1861.

(Chicago Historical Society)

JAMES A. MULLIGAN (1830-1864), the leader of the Chicago Irish Brigade (23d Illinois Volunteers), was stationed in Jefferson City on August 31, 1861, when he received orders to proceed west to hold the town of Lexington. Ten days later, Colonel Mulligan's militia began fortifying the Masonic College and an area of about 18 acres.

(State Historical Society of Missouri)

(State Historical Society of Missouri)

OPPOSITE: On September 12, nearly 3,000 Union soldiers held off an estimated 18,000 Confederate troops at Lexington. Six days later, having cut off the water and food supply to Mulligan's men, Price renewed the attack.

On the morning of September 20, Price's men advanced, protected by impenetrable, moving walls of water-soaked hemp bales. Toward mid-afternoon of the same day, after 52 hours of uninterrupted fighting, Colonel Mulligan surrendered to General Price.

(State Historical Society of Missouri)

(Dr. Joseph S. Summers, Jr.)

A Confederate soldier shoots a Union picket outside Jefferson City in September 1861.

Fremont Hastens to Jefferson City

Meanwhile, Fremont, alarmed that Price might try to move down the Missouri River and seize Jefferson City, left St. Louis with a force totaling almost 15,000 men. Arriving in Jefferson City on September 26, 1861, he dispersed his troops and began frantic construction of trenches and defenses. A sketch from *Harper's Weekly* shows a number of tent camps "dotting the hills and slopes around Jefferson City." Fremont was headquartered at Camp Lillie.

(State Historical Society of Missouri)

The arrival of General Fremont's Division from St. Louis in September 1861.

(State Historical Society of Missouri)

Camp Lillie was General Fremont's Jefferson City headquarters. Although opinions vary as to the camp's exact location, *Harper's Weekly* described it as being "a mile south of the Capitol." Some sources report the encampment was named for Fremont's daughter.

(State Historical Society of Missouri)

Where Was Camp Lillie?

Sometimes, the reconstruction of Civil War facts becomes difficult. For example, the location of General John C. Fremont's headquarters in Jefferson City in late September 1861 is a source of debate among local historians.

Harper's Weekly described Camp Lillie as being "a mile south of the Capitol." That location would indicate the hill on which the public high school now stands.

This position was reaffirmed in an article in the *Jefferson City News Tribune* on April 18, 1971. Jeff Matteson wrote: "His [Fremont's] selection of the Dulle home was a natural. It overlooked his forces camped about a mile east of Camp Lillie and it was one of the most gracious homes in the area."

However, Guy M. Sone, a Jefferson City native and avid historian, wrote a report in 1961 that disagreed with that location. He argued that Camp Lillie was, in fact, located in an area between the Dulle home on St. Mary's Boulevard and the town. He included the following articles to substantiate his theory.

The *St. Louis Weekly Democrat* of September 29, 1861, states: ". . . General Fremont went into camp this morning about half a mile back of town." According to Mr. Sone, Jefferson City in 1861 was built close to the Missouri River. Therefore, "half a mile back of town" meant away from the river.

The *Missouri Republican* dated October 1, 1861, states: "General Fremont is encamped in the southwestern part of the town . . ." This location, Mr. Sone continued, would place the camp very close to the Dulle home, which is in the southwestern part of Jefferson City, and as indicated in the previous paragraph, about a half mile beyond the outskirts of 1861 Jefferson City.

On October 22, 1861, the *St. Louis Weekly Missouri Democrat* ran this item written by a correspondent of the *Cincinnati Gazette*: "If I had been looking for her [Mrs. Jessie Fremont], I should have gone to her quarters some distance up on the hill, expecting to find her comfortably housed for the day." Mr. Sone believed this was in reference to the Dulle home, because at that time the house was surrounded by a two hundred acre farm, and so far as he could ascertain, the most likely house nearby.

It is documented that Jessie Fremont visited her husband at Camp Lillie and that she had "quarters" with her daughter and two sons at a hilltop home, the Gerhard Herman Dulle home. Family legend tells how Mr. and Mrs. Dulle prepared for the arrival of the soldiers by storing their precious quilts and possibly other valuable items in a large trunk and burying it in the yard.

The house, although not the oldest in Jefferson City, is the oldest house continuously occupied by one family.

Headquarters, Jefferson City, Mo., Oct 19 1861.

Officer Picket:

Pass Mrs R[illegible]

out of the City, to St Louis

BY ORDER

Brig. Gen Commandin

(James Jop

An official pass to leave Fremont's headquarters in Jefferson City.

(Cole Co. Historical Society)

The G. H. Dulle home, built in 1858 at 800 St. Mary's Boulevard, was the headquarters of General John C. Fremont during his stay in Jefferson City in late September 1861. Tradition says he held conferences in the sitting room just left of the entry, and had his working desk as well as his bed in the northeast bedroom on the second floor (upper right windows). This room provides a commanding view of the Capitol area.

Troops were stationed at the old fairgrounds in the Fairmount Court area and in the McClung Park area. Artillery projectile fragments found embedded in the McClung Park quarry suggest that the quarry was used for artillery practice. Civil War artifacts such as coins of the period, bullets, mess kits, knives, forks, buttons, buckles and melted down lead have been found by Richard Terry and other members of the Metal Detectors Club in Ellis-Porter Park, McClung Park, the Jefferson City High School area, and along High and East Capitol streets. Other Civil War artifacts have been found in the area of Ramada Inn and south of Sunset Lake.

With 15,000 of Fremont's soldiers inundating Jefferson City, enormous logistical problems ensued. The normal shelter for a soldier in the summertime was a tent. During the Civil War there were three varieties: the Sibley, shaped like a bell supported by an upright center pole; the wedge or A tents (because from the end they looked like a capital A without the crossbar); and third, a shelter tent that became widely known as the "dog tent." (In its most common version, the "dog tent" was a two-man habitation unit formed by buttoning together two half shelters and stretching them over a horizontal pole supported at each end by a pronged stake.) Men accustomed to living in the luxury of a house took unkindly to the constricted and hard living in the "dog tents" and put up derisive signs over their cramped quarters such as "PUPS FOR SALE," "RAT TERRIER HOLE NO. 1," and "SONS OF BITCHES WITHIN." A later version of the tent, the pup tent, was used extensively well into the World War II era. Sibley, wedge, and dog tents are identifiable in the *Harper's Weekly* sketch of Jefferson City.

To feed the thousands of soldiers encamped in Jefferson City was a quartermaster's nightmare. Officers requisitioned wagons from Army supply, and from farms and homes throughout the area, to gather and transport food to feed the troops. Many of the displaced farmers encamped along Wears Creek used their teams of horses and oxen to help in the food gathering effort. In addition, all the shops at the penitentiary were used to produce equipment for the field deployment of troops.

(State Historical Society of Missouri)

This sketch showing breast works thrown up for the defense of Jefferson City appears to have been drawn looking to the northeast from a point just west of Broadway and West Main Street. A poorly proportioned Capitol dome is shown behind the Armory.

Fortifications

There is an old military maxim: "Take and defend the high ground." It was consistently and strenuously practiced by both Union and Confederate commanders during the Civil War. With this knowledge, a look at the U.S. Geological Survey's topographic map of Jefferson City, and with engineer sketches, maps and information of the period, one gets a good idea of where the Civil War defenses were constructed in Jefferson City. This analysis is further confirmed by Civil War artifacts collected by metal detecting enthusiasts.

The construction of defenses of Jefferson City was a stop-start affair and difficult to delineate at any given period. However, it is known that by the time of Price's raid in October 1864, there were three rings of defenses:

1) To protect the Capitol, a long and heavily-fortified palisade bristling with abatis, extended along High Street from the area of St. Peter's School to Cherry Street.

2) The main defenses of Jefferson City were centered on five forts interconnected with long lines of rifle pits, all heavily manned and protected by palisades and *chevaux-de-frise*.

    Miner's Hill - This was the first fort, located on what is now the State of Missouri Surplus Property area (formerly the women's prison). Breastworks with artillery were positioned immediately east of the penitentiary so that covering fire could be directed to steamers on the Missouri River, the Pacific Railroad, and the road leading to St. Louis.

East Fort - Defenses continued south to the present area of the Immaculate Conception Church and along what is now Clark Avenue.

Miller's Hill - This third fort was located along the heights of East Miller Street and Simonsen Jr. High.

Dunklin Fort - Some of the heaviest defenses, however, extended the entire length of the northern side of Dunklin Street (Safeway Store area).

College Hill - The fifth fort was located on the heights of Brooks Street, presently the location of the city waterworks. An 1864 sketch of Jefferson City defenses shows that in addition to the gun battery, 3,000 Union troops were billeted here.

3) Outside the city limits, another line of defense continued:

Southern Hills [area previously unnamed] was along the ridge between Lafayette and Madison Streets, where the Jefferson City High School, the Thorpe Gordon School and the Charles E. Still Osteopathic Hospital now stand.

Koch's Hill was along the heights of Jefferson Street.

Swift's Hill is now the Swift's Highway area.

Doyl's [Dulle's] Hill, located on what is now the St. Mary's Health Center area, completed the third arch of defenses.

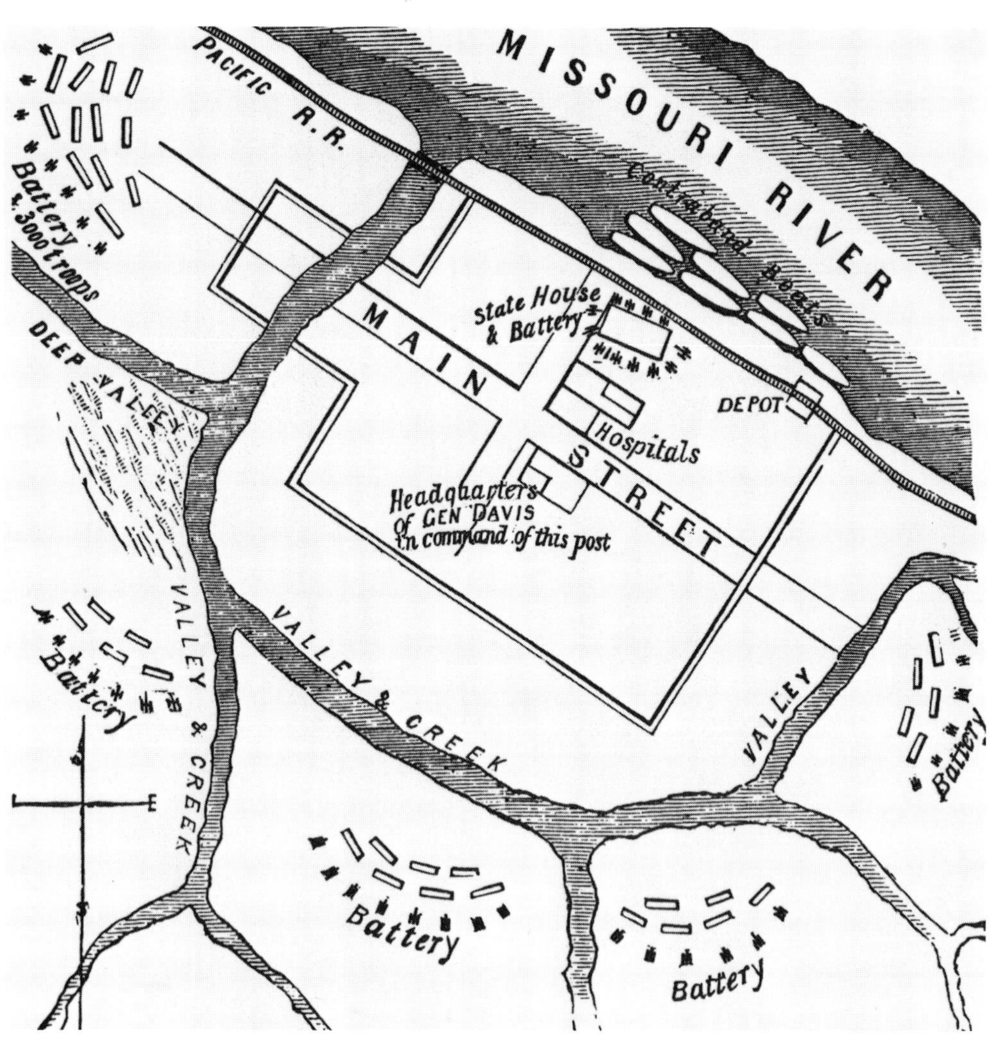

(State Historical Society of Missouri)

The above map (1861) details the perimeters of the defensive lines. As you study this map and the one on the facing page (1864), note the inconsistencies in the locations of the rivers and creeks.

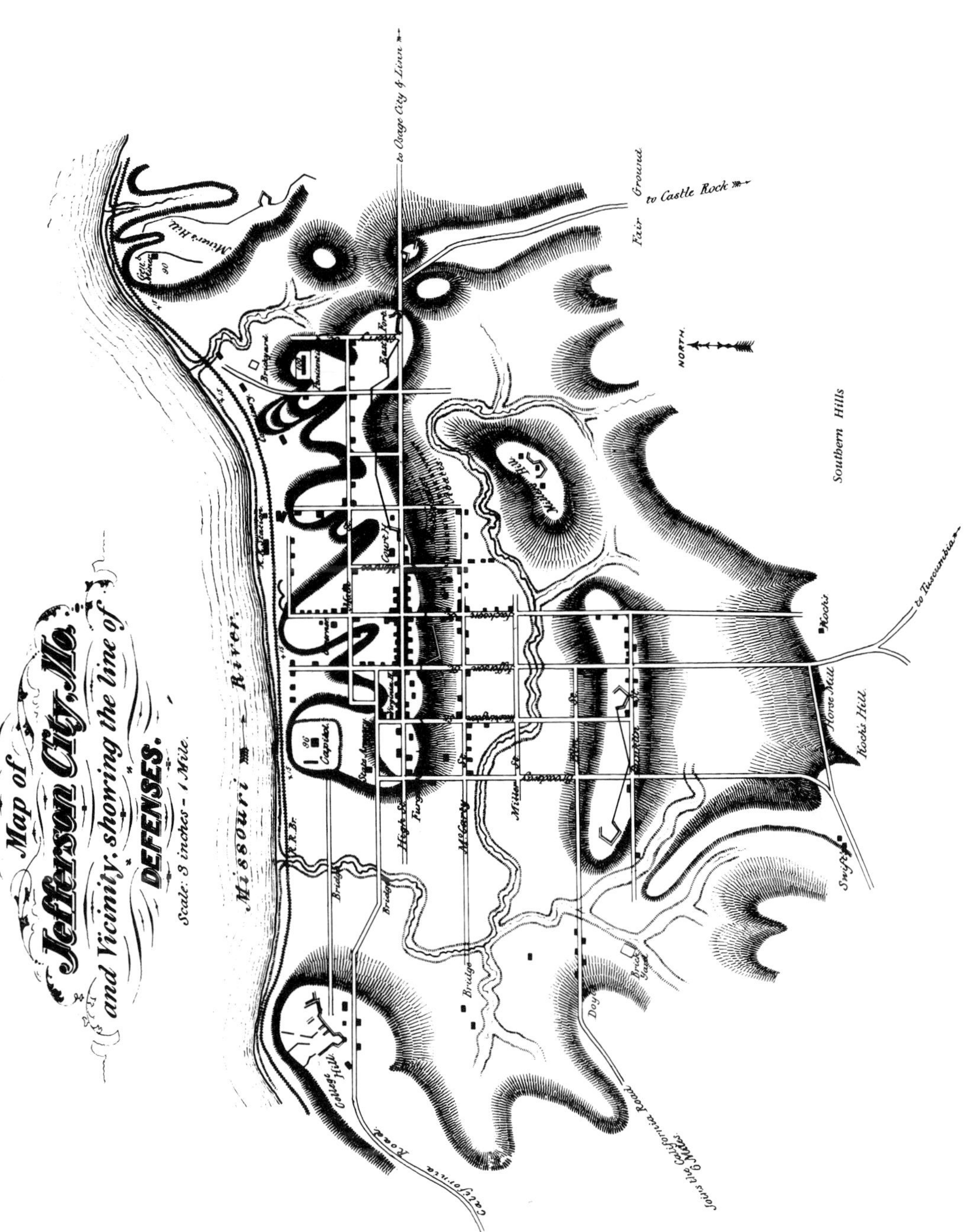

(The National Archives)

Price Heads South

Price was unable to maintain himself at Lexington and on September 30, 1861, he did not march to Jefferson City as Fremont had anticipated, but set out again for southwest Missouri. This time he led a large number of volunteers for the Southern cause.

(State Historical Society of Missouri)

On October 14, 1861, General Fremont arrived at Warsaw, 65 miles southwest of Jefferson City. By using canister shot, his division dispersed a Confederate cavalry force and built a bridge over the Osage River.

Fremont Replaced

Price's leisurely retreat from Lexington gave Frank Blair renewed opportunity to heap blame upon Fremont's exasperatingly inept military administration. He accused Fremont of sacrificing Mulligan at Lexington as he had Lyon the previous month at Wilson's Creek. Fremont reacted by arresting Blair. He then sent his wife, Jessie, to seek an interview with Lincoln to plead his case. Lincoln refused to see her. Later, he relented and met with Mrs. Fremont. The meeting was a stormy one ending in recriminations. Fremont's ill-advised and unauthorized proclamation of emancipation, the military defeats at Wilson's Creek and Lexington, the charges of irregularities in the disbursement of military funds, along with the commissioning of officers of questionable military abilities was too much for Lincoln and he decided to remove him. When Blair was released, he was determined to get revenge in full measure. It was an old Missouri saying that when the Blairs went into a fight, they came out with a funeral. This time a funeral did not result, but Fremont was replaced within five weeks.

In the meantime, Fremont had moved most of his troops from Jefferson City. His army of some 50,000 was distributed in five divisions: General David Hunter's division was headquartered at Versailles, General John Pope went to Boonville, General Franz Sigel to Sedalia, General Alexander S. Asboth to Tipton, and General John McKinstry to Syracuse. He established temporary headquarters in Tipton, supposedly located in the Rose Hill Seminary, now the Maclay House. Troops were bivouacked on lands where the fairground is presently located. A sketch from *Harper's Weekly* dated November 2, 1861, shows the tents and wagons for some 10,000 troops.

Fremont arrived in Springfield on October 27, 1861, in pursuit of General Price. Six days later, before his vision of victory could become a reality, he was relieved of his command.

MAJOR GENERAL DAVID HUNTER (1802-1886) replaced General Fremont as commander of the Department of the West on November 2, 1861. Fremont had held the position for 122 days. The Western Department was reorganized shortly thereafter, and on November 19, Major General Henry W. Halleck superseded Hunter as the commander.

(State Historical Society of Missouri)

Part III

War 1862

Armies Withdraw

Harper's Weekly Domestic Intelligence

During the first three months of 1862, correspondents for *Harper's Weekly* reported several items of interest relating to central Missouri. Although there was considerable trouble from the bushwhackers and guerrillas during the remainder of 1862, no major military action was reported in the area.

January 11, 1862: General Price flees through Springfield to Arkansas, burning bridges behind them, including General Fremont's new bridge over the Osage [at Warsaw].

The rebels continue their depredations on the North Missouri Railroad. They burned another train on the 28th and they boast they will destroy every car on the road.

February 8, 1862: Accounts indefinite, but Price probably still in retreat. . . General Price wrote General Halleck asking if he intended to hang bridge burners and received an affirmative reply.

February 15, 1862: The rebel General Price remains at Springfield. Another terrible battle anticipated unless he withdraws.

General Halleck has seized ex-Governor Claiborne F. Jackson's hemp plantation in Saline County for confiscation.

March 1, 1862: Price driven out of Missouri. On 14th, from General Halleck to General McClellan, a dispatch announcing the rebel General Price, with his whole army, evacuated Springfield on Wednesday night. On 16th, intelligence received that Price's rear guard was overtaken, and after a short resistance fled and dispersed, leaving in the hands of our troops more prisoners than they could well care for, and deserting all their wagons and baggage on the road.

March 8, 1862: General Curtis has driven the rebel army 65 miles south into Arkansas. Brigadier-General Price, brother of the rebel chief, and several officers of his staff were captured.

The Horsemen

They bore many titles: bushwhackers, guerrillas, night riders, marauders, irregulars, raiders and murderers. They brought to Missouri a most unpleasant chapter of unceasing, blatant, and purposeful ruthlessness. They appeared suddenly, overwhelmed an unprotected and defenseless adversary, robbed and pillaged, and very often committed brutal murder. They rode with a black flag emblazoned with the skull and cross bones, or the word "death," and their battle cry was "kill." Links to the formal forces of the military, where they existed at all, were tenuous at best. Operating under the pretense of a higher authority, they were unscrupulous men who had longed for the opportunity to prey on their neighbors. Robbing their neighbors of personal belongings, seizing horses, cattle and booty, they frequently repaired to a predetermined sanctuary and defiantly sold their booty at auction. When innocent people could not be found to plunder, bushwhackers often preyed upon one another.

Intolerant, arrogant, insensitive, driven for wealth and power — four of the most lawless Confederate guerrilla leaders in Missouri were William C. Quantrill, William C. "Bloody Bill" Anderson, David Poole and George Todd. Quantrill had been commissioned a colonel in the Confederate Army while Anderson and Todd held the rank of captain.

The Union had its own band of guerrillas. The western border of Missouri was infested with bands of robbers from Kansas known as "Red Legs." The "Jayhawkers" conducted raids into Missouri ostensibly for the purpose of striking at slavery, but once inside the state, they too committed acts of robbery, arson and murder.

The Confederate guerrilla bands befuddled the Federal high command, harassed occupation troops, disrupted supply and communication lines, and attacked convoys of troops and supplies en route to Union garrisons. These gangs also kept the Federals from getting accurate information on Confederate forces. The bushwhackers, as time passed, perfected hit-and-run tactics, ambush and terrorism, and then in classic guerrilla fashion melted back into the civilian population.

Having suffered considerable losses in men and supplies, the Federals resorted to both direct and indirect challenge to the Confederate dominance of the Missouri countryside. During the first two years of war, the Confederates rode circles around the

(State Historical Society of Missouri)

WILLIAM CLARK QUANTRILL (1837-1865), a school teacher from Ohio, was a friend of the slaveholding citizens of western Missouri. Quantrill was notorious during 1862-1865 for his leadership of the cold-blooded, calculated guerrilla warfare against the Union.

Yankee horsemen. A British observer wrote that the Yankees "could scarcely sit on their horses even when trotting." Union leaders, conscious of their own deficiencies, began an elaborate cavalry training program. They armed their troopers with seven-shot repeating carbines which not only gave them a margin over their Confederate counterparts but allowed them to fight dismounted against infantry troops. The increased firepower, improved horsemanship, competent leadership, and added experience quickly brought the Union cavalry up to par with the Confederates. The Union troopers were not only willing but itching to do battle with the Confederates.

The Federals also began using indirect methods to stop the Confederate marauders — by imprisoning or exiling friends and families who provided the Confederate guerrillas with weapons, information, shelter or sustenance. Among those arrested were Jesse and Frank James' mother and sister, three sisters of "Bloody Bill" Anderson and relatives of Cole Younger. They were imprisoned in an old brick building on Grand Avenue between Fourteenth and Fifteenth streets in Kansas City. A section of the building collapsed killing one of Anderson's sisters and a cousin of Cole Younger. Believing that his sister's death was attributable to Union troops, "Bloody Bill" carried a silken cord, and added a knot for every Yankee he exterminated in revenge for the death of his sister. It was said that when he died he had several hundred knots in the cord.

These acts provoked even more virulent hatreds. The treachery became more odious, and as the scale of operations increased, the

(State Historical Society of Missouri)

"BLOODY BILL" ANDERSON (1837-1864) is described by Richard Brownlee in *Gray Ghosts of the Confederacy*: "Anderson became insane because of the injury to his sisters, and his attitude toward all men who supported or served the Union was that of a homicidal maniac."

ferocity of pillaging, burning and murder intensified. There were few voices of moderation and caution. Passions were unleashed on both sides to get full measure of reprisal — eye for an eye, a tooth for a tooth. Murder and desecration of bodies were committed with impassivity and impunity of judgment and punishment. Divided, Jefferson City became a community of seething intrigues. Bushwhackers operated with impunity not only in Cole County but in the surrounding counties as well. There were a number of instances in the Jefferson City area of people being robbed and farms being burned. Bushwhackers fired on trains coming to Jefferson City, and they robbed stages carrying mail and passengers to Boonville and Columbia.

Part IV

War 1863

Emancipation

(State Historical Society of Missouri)

Thousands of slaves moved north after the signing of the Emancipation Proclamation.

On January 1, 1863, Lincoln issued his Emancipation Proclamation which freed slaves in states that were in rebellion against the Union. It did not, however, affect the border states such as Missouri, Kentucky, Maryland, and Delaware, nor did it affect Tennessee and parts of Louisiana and Virginia inasmuch as they were not in a state of rebellion at that time.

In June 1863, Governor Gamble called a convention in Jefferson City on the subject of emancipation and stated that some scheme should be adopted whereby the slaves of Missouri would also be set free. There were the "Radicals" who favored immediate emancipa-

(State Historical Society of Missouri)

ABRAHAM LINCOLN (1809-1865), 16th president of the United States, signed the Emancipation Proclamation on January 1, 1863. As it lay unrolled before him, Mr. Lincoln took a pen and said, "I have been shaking hands since nine o'clock this morning and my right arm is almost paralyzed. If my name ever goes into history, it will be for this act, and my whole soul is in it. If my hand trembles when I sign the Proclamation, all who examine the document hereafter will say, 'He hesitated.'" He then took up the pen, and slowly and firmly signed his name.

tion and this group included many Germans. The "Conservatives" were in favor of gradual emancipation. The convention passed an ordinance providing: "Slavery and involuntary servitude except for punishment of crime should cease to exist on July 4, 1870, and that all slaves within the State on that date should be declared free." This brought a split between the Radicals and the Conservatives, prompting the Radicals to call a mass meeting in Jefferson City and promulgate an indictment that a "Committee of Seventy" carried to President Lincoln. On September 30, 1863, Lincoln received the Committee and listened to their recommendations for immediate emancipation in Missouri and other grievances, but refused to support them. The Radicals, incensed, stated they would refuse to support Lincoln for re-election.

Reynolds Moves Government-in-Exile

After Governor Jackson developed pneumonia and died near Little Rock on December 6, 1862, Lieutenant Governor Thomas C. Reynolds was recalled from a self-imposed retirement in his native South Carolina. On February 14, 1863, he issued a proclamation of Jackson's death and his own assumption to power. In late June 1863, Reynolds transferred the government-in-exile from Camden to Little Rock, Arkansas. When that city was threatened by Union forces, he moved south, first to Arkadelphia then to Washington, Arkansas. From there the capital-in-exile was moved to Shreveport, Louisiana, and finally established at Marshall, Texas, where it remained until the end of the war.

THOMAS CAUTE REYNOLDS (1821-1887) was elected Missouri's lieutenant governor in 1860. He fled south with Governor Jackson in 1861, and upon Jackson's death, became Missouri's governor-in-exile in Marshall, Texas.

(Walker-Missouri Resources Division)

(State Historical Society of Missouri)

The home of Judge Asa Willie in Marshall, Texas, became Missouri's capitol-in-exile.

(State Historical Society of Missouri)

Across the street from the Willie home, the residence of Mrs. Mary Key was leased and became the governor's mansion.

Order Number 11

The guerrilla bands grew in size and complexity of operations. Lawrence, Kansas, founded by New England abolitionists, was the center of Jayhawker and Red Legs raids on Missouri border towns. Slaves were taken, and property seized on these raids was openly sold or distributed to the population.

(State Historical Society of Missouri)

Lawrence had become a hated symbol to Confederate fighters, and on August 21, 1863, Quantrill, riding with more than 300 men, wheeled out of Missouri and wreaked fearful vengeance on that town. Quantrill admonished his men to "kill every male and burn every house in Lawrence." By the time he left Lawrence, every house was in flames and 183 males had been murdered in cold blood.

In retribution for the Quantrill raid, Union General Thomas Ewing issued his notorious Order Number 11. By terms of this order, all persons living in certain areas of the Missouri counties of Jackson, Cass, Bates, and parts of Vernon were given 15 days to vacate their homes. Their homes, barns and fields were put to the torch. Over 10,000 people were made homeless and the term "burnt district" would be applied to Bates and Cass Counties for years to come. A colonel serving on the staff of General Ewing begged the general in vain not to implement the order. He later painted the scene of terror. His name was George Caleb Bingham.

In the fall of 1863, Anderson broke with Quantrill to form his own guerrilla band. Frank and Jesse James, George and Tom Todd, David Poole and Archie Clements rode with him into Missouri.

OPPOSITE: William Quantrill considered Lawrence, Kansas, the center of all his troubles. On August 21, 1863, his guerrillas rode into the town of 2,000 and in two hours left behind a devastated, burning city.

THOMAS J. EWING, JR. (1829-1896) headed the District of the Border in western Missouri/eastern Kansas. It was at Senator Jim Lane's insistence after the raid on Lawrence, Kansas, that General Ewing drew up and enforced Order No. 11.

(State Historical Society of Missouri)

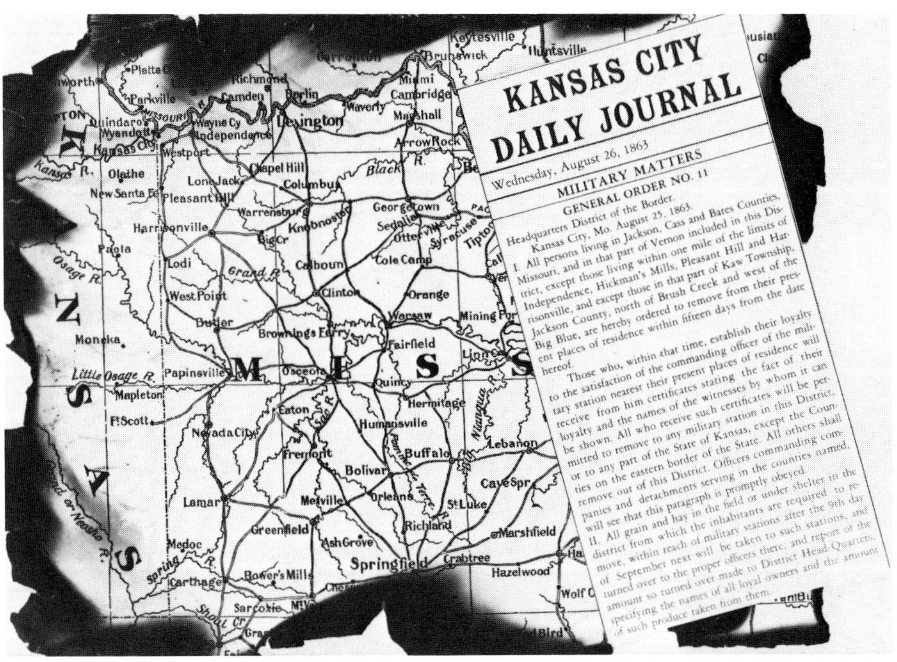

KANSAS CITY DAILY JOURNAL

Wednesday, August 26, 1863

MILITARY MATTERS

GENERAL ORDER NO. 11

Headquarters District of the Border.
Kansas City, Mo. August 25, 1863.

I. All persons living in Jackson, Cass and Bates Counties, Missouri, and in that part of Vernon included in this District, except those living within one mile of the limits of Independence, Hickman's Mills, Pleasant Hill and Harrisonville, and except those in that part of Kaw Township, Jackson County, north of Brush Creek and west of the Big Blue, are hereby ordered to remove from their present places of residence within fifteen days from the date hereof.

Those who, within that time, establish their loyalty to the satisfaction of the commanding officer of the military station nearest their present places of residence will receive from him certificates stating the fact of their loyalty and the names of the witnesses by whom it can be shown. All who receive such certificates will be permitted to remove to any military station in this District, or to any part of the State of Kansas, except the Counties on the eastern border of the State. All others shall remove out of this District. Officers commanding companies and detachments serving in the counties named, will see that this paragraph is promptly obeyed.

II. All grain and hay in the field or under shelter in the district from which the inhabitants are required to remove, within reach of military stations after the 9th day of September next will be taken to such stations, and turned over to the proper officers there, and report of the amount so turned over made to District Head-Quarters, specifying the names of all loyal owners and the amount of such produce taken from them.

(State Historical Society of Missouri)

(State Historical Society of Missouri)

"Order No. 11" was painted by George Caleb Bingham. General Thomas Ewing is depicted in the center enforcing the decree.

(State Historical Society of Missouri)

Hangings were common during the warfare on the border.

Price Sends Shelby North

Jefferson City was threatened again in the fall of 1863. Union forces sent into Arkansas had captured Little Rock. To relieve the pressure on his forces, Price detached General Joseph O. Shelby, often described as "the best cavalry general of the South." He gave Shelby a brigade from Marmaduke's cavalry division along with a battery of light artillery to stage a raid into Missouri with hope that this diversion would cause the withdrawal of at least part of the Union troops then in the Arkansas Valley.

Raid on Tipton

Shelby started out on September 22, 1863, with upwards of 2,000 men. With scarcely any opposition, he rapidly moved north capturing Neosho and a detachment of Home Guard before heading for his goal, Jefferson City. Shelby, a Missourian, had stated it was his desire to fly the stars and bars over the state Capitol. Passing through Sarcoxie, Bowers Mill, Stockton and Warsaw, he moved on to Tipton. At Tipton on October 10, Shelby struck with vengeance. A small garrison made token resistance but fled before the Rebel onslaught. Shelby's troops burned the depot, set fire to a large number of freight and passenger cars, plundered the city, and tore up the tracks for miles on either side of town. His planned move to Jefferson City was canceled when Shelby learned from Confederate

(State Historical Society of Missouri)

JOSEPH ORVILLE SHELBY (1830-1897) served with the Confederate army throughout the war. He advanced through the ranks from colonel to brigadier general, leading his troops several times into Missouri.

spies that Union troops were being rushed to Jefferson City under the command of General E.B. Brown.

Meanwhile, when word of the attack on Tipton reached Jefferson City, panic ensued. Union soldiers were again encamped on the hills of Jefferson City, and troops frantically refurbished the defensive fortifications about the city. Union sympathizers in the city, fearing that their homes and the city would be put to the Confederate torch, breathed a sigh of relief when it was learned that Shelby had gone to Boonville.

Boonville, a hotbed of Confederate support, greeted Shelby warmly and assured him of their Southern loyalty and support. Hundreds of recruits had joined Shelby, and his column was lengthened by three hundred wagons drawn by captured mules and horses. Shelby began a hasty retreat after being attacked by Union cavalry at Marshall. The Tipton raid was unique in that it lasted longer and covered greater distance than had yet been accomplished by any body of horsemen from either army in the entire course of the war.

The Unsung Hero

All too often, people who affect the course of a nation are lost from the pages of history. A century ago John Newman Edwards was known nationwide as a controversial newspaper editor, writer and Confederate soldier, and yet today few books include any information about this colorful character.

Two sources have been uncovered. An article written on October 24, 1961, by Herb Rice for the *Kansas City Times* was located in the files of the Cole County Historical Society. It describes this native Virginian, born in Front Royal on January 4, 1839. John Newman Edwards moved to Missouri as a teenager and settled in the Lexington area, where he later became the editor of the militant and highly influential weekly, *The Expositor.*

At the outbreak of the Civil War, Edwards joined the Iron Brigade, a contingent of Missouri Southern patriots organized by his Lexington County friend, Joseph Orville Shelby. He was appointed a brigadier-adjutant, with the rank of major. As the adjutant, his job was to write the official report of the action of the cavalry unit. His mastery of the English language and his flamboyant writing style are a trademark of his routine reports. In 1863 in Cape Girardeau, Edwards was wounded, captured and confined to prison.

Immediately after the war, John Edwards rode to Mexico with Shelby, and for two years edited the English language *Mexican Times* for the former Confederate soldiers in Mexico. Later, he became co-founder of the *Kansas City Times*, and authored three books: *Shelby and His Men or the War in the West*, *Noted Guerrillas* and *Shelby's Expedition to Mexico.*

According to William Settle's *Jesse James Was His Name*, when Edwards was a Jefferson City correspondent for the *Kansas City Times*, he wrote many articles defending Jesse and Frank James, and did more than any other individual to create the Robin Hood myth that surrounded these two outlaws. After Jesse was killed, it was John N. Edwards who arranged for Frank James to surrender, and accompanied him to Jefferson City to meet with Governor Crittenden.

John Newman Edwards fought for the Southern cause and wrote praise for the Southern leaders. He is one of many forgotten heroes.

Part V

War 1864

Centralia Massacre

On September 27, 1864, an unruly group of 80 strangers rode into Centralia, Missouri. Some wore Union uniforms, others wore linen dusters. A number carried four or five quick firing Navy Colt revolvers in their belts. On signal, the group rode through the town firing their weapons and chasing the fleeing civilians. In the midst of this mayhem was their leader, the 24-year-old William "Bloody Bill" Anderson.

In appearance Anderson was sinister, with a head too large for the body that supported it. Anderson's men, brandishing their guns, entered private homes and public stores and looted and robbed the occupants of their personal valuables and saleable goods. A dry goods store was plundered of its shoes, boots and clothing. A number of men gathered about a barrel of whiskey that had been appropriated from one of the stores. Wild carousing and sporadic firing of guns continued until a stagecoach came into town. It was quickly surrounded and the eight passengers were asked to surrender all their valuables and the money they were carrying. One of the eight men was James S. Rollins, a U.S. representative (Democrat) and the "father" of the University of Missouri.

At 11:30 a.m., a train came into the Centralia station and was immediately surrounded by Anderson's gang. As the passengers were marched off, each one was accosted by a bushwhacker who demanded money and valuables. Other bushwhackers plundered the baggage cars. Aboard the train were twenty-two unarmed Union soldiers, most of whom were wounded or on sick leave from their units. The outlaws swarmed aboard the train. After the soldiers were robbed and stripped of their uniforms, they were marched to the station, lined up, and killed with a single shot to the skull. Only one was spared, a Union sergeant who Anderson hoped to exchange for one of his men that the Union troops had captured. Some of the bodies were scalped. Others were placed on the tracks and run over by the locomotive. The rail cars were set afire and the locomotive's throttle was locked, sending the train hurtling unattended down the tracks to crash at Sturgeon.

Two hours later, Union Major A.V.E. Johnson with 147 men of Companies A, G, and H of the Thirty-ninth Missouri Volunteer Infantry saw the smoke coming from Centralia and hurried to investigate. They had been patrolling for bushwhackers in Monroe County east of Centralia. Told of Anderson's raid, and despite warnings that some 400 of Anderson's men were encamped outside town, Johnson pursued the gang. Meanwhile, Anderson had split his troopers into three groups forming an "open box" and waited for Johnson to walk into the trap. They didn't wait long, for Johnson brought his untrained men against some of the best horsemen in the nation. On signal, screaming Rebels streamed from three sides and fell upon the Federal volunteers, stampeding their horses and killing most where they stood. Johnson was felled by a ball to the temple. Some historians say it was delivered by 17-year-old Jesse James. Those Union soldiers who attempted to escape were pursued and unmercifully shot down. The bodies were brought to Centralia. Seventy-nine unclaimed bodies were buried in a mass grave on the eastern section of Centralia. On December 17, 1873, they were disinterred and reinterred in the Jefferson City National Cemetery. Today at the cemetery, an 8-foot obelisk sits atop a gentle slope. On three sides are etched the names of the Missouri and Iowa farmboys who died that day. On one side there is an inscription which reads, "The remains of the members of Companies A,G, and H, 39 Regiment, Missouri Volunteer Infantry who were killed at Centralia, Mo. on 27th day of September 1864 are interred here." There is no mention of the word massacre nor of the perpetrator, as though it had not happened or, maybe, so the world could forget the brutality and barbarity that occurred in central Missouri on that day so long ago.

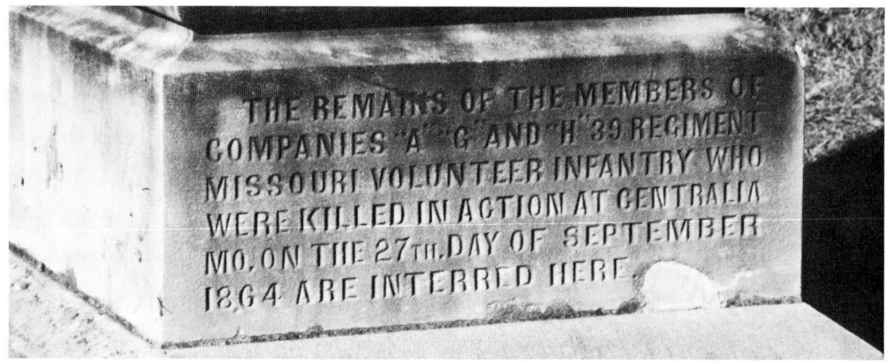

(Dr. Joseph S. Summers, Jr.)

(Dr. Joseph S. Summers, Jr.)

OPPOSITE AND ABOVE: A tombstone honors the Union soldiers who were brutally murdered in 1864 in Centralia, Missouri, by "Bloody Bill" Anderson's guerrillas. The memorial stands in the National Cemetery in Jefferson City.

The Final Days

Price Heads North Again

Lee was staggering at Petersburg, Virginia, under heavy and incessant blows, Johnson had been removed from command of the Army of the Tennessee, Sherman was marching through Georgia, and Hood was desperately trying to hold Tennessee. During 1864, Price had ordered several raids into Union territory. The spoils from these raids supplied Price's army with "transportation, small arms, camp equipage and ammunition to load 300 wagons." That fall, Price hurled his army northward in heroic desperation to retrieve the fortunes of a dying Confederacy. He had been assured that a diversion into Missouri would cause full rebellion by all those organizations opposed to the Union. Price was relying heavily on the Southern underground or Copperhead organization, known in Missouri by various names but chiefly as "The Knights of the Golden Circle." Price was also hopeful that thousands of new recruits would join his army.

So the mules and horses were shod, ammunition issued and rations allotted. With three divisions commanded by Generals Joseph Shelby, John S. Marmaduke, and James Fagan, an army of more than 12,000 Confederates entered the southeast corner of Missouri on September 23, 1864, ostensibly to attack St. Louis.

(State Historical Society of Missouri)

General Thomas J. Ewing, Jr. (author of the infamous Order No. 11) was transferred across the state to Pilot Knob in Iron County to defend Ft. Davidson against Price's army.

Battle of Pilot Knob

The forward elements of Price's army reached Pilot Knob on the afternoon of September 26 and skirmishes developed. Units of Federal cavalry were sent out to harass Price's line of march. On September 27, General Thomas Ewing's force of around 1,000 men was forced back and waited behind their fortifications for Price's main force to attack. Price attacked during the afternoon of the 27th, but the Union forces had 11 artillery pieces well placed and repulsed every attack. By evening General Ewing realized that he could not hold out against a superior force, and shortly after midnight, his troops slipped out (caisson and artillery wheels were muffled with tents and blankets), then blew up the fort's powder magazine. When Price took the fort, more than 1,000 of his crack soldiers lay dead or wounded.

A correspondent from *Harper's Weekly* gave this account in the October 22, 1864, issue:

"The Invasion of Missouri"

> Brig. General Ewing has arrived in Rolla. We are able to give a detailed account of his defense of Pilot Knob. He reached the post on September 25, and with a garrison of 1,000 men undertook to hold his ground against Price's far superior force. The position is entirely indefensible, as it is surrounded on all sides by elevations which command it. General Price attempted an advance into the valley, and was terribly beaten, but gaining the mountain sides, he compelled Ewing to evacuate. On the way to Rolla, Ewing was surrounded and came near capture. He escaped, however, by the aid of forces sent to his assistance. On the 7th, the rebels made a demonstration against Jefferson City, but this proved only a feint to occupy our forces while they crossed the Osage River. During the night, they pressed westward. Price's army is estimated at 20,000 strong, with from 16 to 25 cannon. On the morning of the 8th, General Pleasonton arrived, and assuming command, followed the rebels with about 8,000 cavalry.

Confederate Forces Advance to Jefferson City

After a feint toward St. Louis and finding it heavily defended, and following the futile chase of General Ewing by Shelby and Marmaduke, Price turned his forces westward toward his secondary objective, Jefferson City.

At the capital city, Governor-in-exile Thomas C. Reynolds, who rode with Price as an aide to General Shelby, would assume the position of governor-in-residence and establish a Confederate stewardship of the state. Larger possibilities loomed. The North was war weary. If Price could inflict a serious defeat in the heartland of the Union and reclaim Missouri for the Confederacy, the result might lead to a negotiated peace on the basis of Southern independence. Price, however, was bitterly disappointed at the meager turnout of new recruits, and the rebellion and popular support he had counted upon did not materialize.

Guerrilla forces were given orders to disrupt rail communications and to draw on the wealth of the land to supply and refit the army. During the first week of October, "Bloody Bill" Anderson attacked several trains of the North Missouri Railroad, also known as the Hannibal and St. Joseph Railroad (now the Burlington Route), robbed the passengers and committed other depredations.

Between September 29 and October 1, the three divisions of Price's army divided. While Generals Shelby and Fagan moved northwest and cut off several miles of the southwestern branch of the Pacific Railroad and burned the depot at Cuba, forces

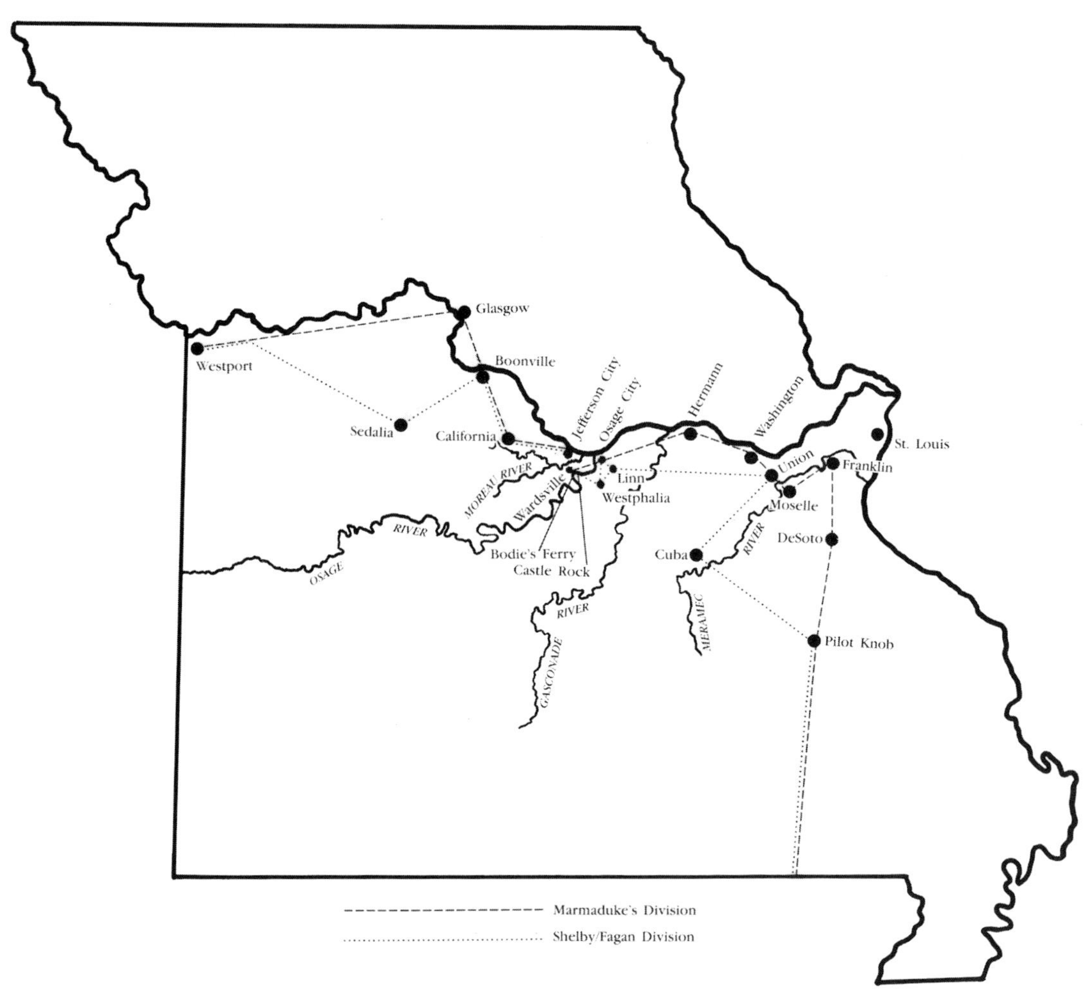

(Dr. Joseph S. Summers, Jr.)

The map of the fall campaign of 1864 shows Major General Sterling Price's route that took him through central Missouri and Jefferson City.

under General Marmaduke marched north and destroyed the depot at DeSoto and tore up portions of the track east of Franklin. Marmaduke's division then turned west and destroyed the bridge over the Meramec River at Moselle, and attacked and captured the town of Union, where Price's army reunited.

From Union the army again divided. Shelby and Fagan headed west toward Jefferson City, and Marmaduke marched northwest.

A brigade of Marmaduke's division took possession of the town of Washington on October 2, and two days later, captured a long Pacific Railroad train loaded with ammunition at Miller's Station. With the ammunition and other captured booty, Price's wagon train had swollen to over 500 wagons. That same day, October 4, Marmaduke's forces destroyed the railroad bridge over the Gasconade River and took possession of Hermann before marching west through the river valley forests.

Shelby Crosses the Osage

After leaving Union, Shelby's men stormed into Linn on October 4, captured its garrison of 100 Union troops and, according to *Shelby and His Men*, "struck terror into the Dutch and militia, surprised almost into idiocy."

Forces under Colonel David Shanks burned the large bridge over the Osage River at Osage City. Built nine years earlier by the Pacific

Railroad, the bridge was 1,122 feet long with six wooden spans and one wooden draw span. Shanks then proceeded to Westphalia, where he reunited with Shelby. They took the town, drove out its garrison of one regiment, and, in the process, took many prisoners.

On October 6, General Price ordered Shelby to move forward and force a passage over the Osage River. Shelby's troops advanced with the confidence of veterans. At a ford southeast of Wardsville at the settlement of Castle Rock, Colonel Anderson Gordon's forces attacked and drove the Federals back toward Jefferson City. William Bodie, owner of Bodie's Ferry, was captured. After stripping his farm of livestock and personal property, his captors released him.

At the same time, another brigade of Shelby's division under Colonel Shanks was crossing the Osage River six miles below Castle Rock at Bolton Shoals. Although this passage of the Osage was also successful, Colonel Shanks and a number of Shelby's men were killed.

That night Shelby's division camped six miles south of Jefferson City and waited for Generals Fagan and Marmaduke to join him. General Price, having been notified of the crossing of the Osage, also advanced during the night.

Differences in Historical Accounts

Depending on the research source used, some Civil War events are described from completely different viewpoints. The "burning" of Hermann, Missouri, is a good example.

Harper's History of the Great Rebellion describes the account: ". . .Price, on the 1st of October, after burning the railroad bridge across the Meramac at Moselle, turned toward Jefferson City, having crossed the Gasconade and the Osage by the 6th, burning Herman[n], and the railroad bridge on his way."

Samuel F. Harrison's *History of Hermann, Missouri* presents quite a different interpretation: ". . .As the army [Price's] approached Hermann, it was met by a cannon shot. The army quickly took cover, then another shot came from a second hill and finally a third shot from still another hill. Price was completely fooled, he thought he had met a strong army. Price knew it had to be an army because the only people left in town were women, children, and a few old men, since the younger men had all joined the Union army. After some time of silence from the town, a party was sent to find out about the attack. They found nothing but a small cannon. As it turned out, the cannon was manned by a few old men who had received training in the German Army. They fled the town along with the women and children as soon as the shots were fired. Being in a hurry to get to Jefferson City, the only revenge taken by the Confederates was throwing the cannon into the river."

And the *Hermann Sesquicentennial* tells yet another story: "On the afternoon of October 4th, 1864. . .General Marmaduke's army in the march westward made its appearance on the hills on the east side of town. The town which maintained a militia company composed of infantry and also a section of artillery had received before the war from Gov. Stewart a cannon, and this. . .a handful of desperate citizens picked up and from the railroad track at the high school fired at the intruders who were coming around what is now Frank's Bluff. . .The Confederates figured that all the western hills in town were fortified with artillery and checked their advance for an hour or more. The gun had in the meantime been spiked and thrown in the river. . .The cannon was later fished out of the river by some soldiers and taken to Jefferson City, but again restored to the town by Gov. Gamble."

Federals Fortify the Capital

GENERAL WILLIAM STARKE ROSECRANS (1819–1898) was commander of the Department of the Missouri in 1864. He ordered more than 9,500 troops to reinforce the 7,000 Union soldiers who were fortifying Jefferson City.

(State Historical Society of Missouri)

Price's slow progress toward Jefferson City allowed the Union militia and regular troops to reinforce the city. Hundreds of soldiers and civilians frantically began to refurbish old defenses and construct new ones.

Jefferson City's defenses at the time consisted of five earthen forts, along with lines of connecting rifle pits, heavily protected by palisades and *chevaux-de-frise*. Riflemen were also positioned at portals cut into the walls of the homes along the city's southern perimeter.

General William S. Rosecrans, commander of the Department of the Missouri, was determined not to allow the state capital to fall into the hands of the Confederates, and ordered General John B. Sandborn, commanding the District of the Southwest at Springfield, and General John McNeil, commanding the District of Rolla, to march to the defense of Jefferson City with the least possible delay. In addition, General Clinton B. Fisk, commanding the District of North Missouri at St. Joseph, and General E.B. Brown, commanding the Central District at Warrensburg, were also ordered to send to Jefferson City all the militia that could be spared from their respective districts. In all, over 7,000 troops had gathered in Jefferson City and prepared to defend it once again. In addition to the guns already emplaced in the defenses of the city, the incoming troops brought an additional eight artillery pieces. General Joseph Mower's 5,000 strong veteran division at Cape Girardeau, and General Andrew J. Smith's command from St. Louis with 4,500 men, along with Colonel E.F. Winslow's cavalry were ordered to proceed forthwith to Jefferson City.

Units of the Second Colorado Cavalry boarded the steamer *Benton*, and three companies of the Forty-third Infantry Missouri Volunteers were put aboard the steamer *Westwind*, at Ft. Leavenworth and ordered to proceed to Jefferson City. General Curtis, at Fort Leavenworth, Kansas, fearing that Price would seek vengeance in Kansas, ordered that "the entire militia forces be called out with their best arms and ammunition for a period of thirty days. Each man should be provided with two blankets or a buffalo robe for comfort, and a haversack for carrying provisions. No change of clothing is necessary." Farmers along the routes of march toward Jefferson City were asked to provide the moving armies with provisions and forage for the horses and mules.

Most of the Union troops defending Jefferson City were cavalrymen described by one of Shelby's men as "militia, utterly worthless for sober fighting." Because all available troops had been sent to Jefferson City, the surrounding countryside was left to the mercy of bushwhackers. Citizens, remembering the Centralia massacre the week before, panicked. Male residents of Columbia were ordered to report with the family musket to a newly-constructed blockhouse. Many ignored the order and, instead, loaded their movable property into wagons and followed the Union soldiers to Jefferson City. Left alone, the farm women feared that their homes would be plundered and burned by the bushwhackers. They packed their few belongings and with their children hid in the surrounding forests. Animals left in the fields bellowed for food and milking.

General Pleasonton Commands Union Troops

(State Historical Society of Missouri)

GENERAL ALFRED PLEASONTON (1824–1897), an experienced soldier of many Civil War battles, was ordered by General Grant to take command of the Union army forming in Jefferson City in early October 1864.

General Grant gave command of the army forming in Jefferson City to General Alfred Pleasonton, who had distinguished himself as a cavalry leader in Virginia. General Pleasonton, then in St. Louis, began his march toward Jefferson City. In General Pleasonton, the Union had a commander skilled at organization, with a full and violent commitment to combat. Like Marmaduke, he was a bachelor and a West Point graduate. He had participated in the great battles of the Civil War — South Mountain, Antietam, Fredericksburg and

Chancellorsville. At the Battle of Gettysburg, he had commanded all the Union cavalry.

Among the units ordered to Jefferson City from the east that evening was the notorious Seventh Kansas Jayhawker Regiment. In its ranks stood a young recruit named William Cody, who on a drunken spree had enlisted at Leavenworth. In later years, he gained notoriety as "Buffalo Bill."

Price Enters Jefferson City

On the morning of October 7, General Fagan advanced on a large Union force about five miles from Jefferson City. As the Confederates reached Federal outposts along the Moreau River at Berry Springs, severe fighting broke out between Rebel and Union troops. A number of Fagan's officers and men were killed before the Federals scurried back to their prepared defenses.

With the river area secured, a ragged host of men in butternut and gray splashed across the Moreau and approached the outskirts of the city. Standing on the rooftops of their homes, Jefferson Citians saw moving streams of horses, wagons and men straggling toward their city. Within the city, people were thronging and hurrying to get away from the environs of the Capitol, which was considered a certain target for artillery bombardment. Traffic increased on streets leading westward out of the city.

By noon, Confederate forces occupied the hills to the south and east of the city. The Capitol, with the stars and stripes waving atop its dome, was in plain sight of the Confederates. A battle line about three or four miles long was formed south of the city with Marmaduke deployed to the right and Shelby on the left. Exhausted, bewhiskered Confederate soldiers, with dust-covered faces and eyes laden with fatigue, along with teamsters and the wagon train, came plodding up what is now Green Berry Road. Price unlimbered his artillery, placed it in battery line and readied it for firing on the Capitol defenses. The forward units of Price's army reached Moreau Drive and Hough Park Road. A Union spy in the Confederate ranks watched and carefully noted Price's activity. His name was James Butler Hickok. He later became known as "Wild Bill."

With night approaching, Price decided to encamp his forces two miles south of Jefferson City.

Price then sent Shelby instructions to destroy several bridges, telegraph lines and sections of the railroad west of Jefferson City in the direction of California. Shelby sent a large cavalry force under the command of Lieutenent Colonel McDaniel to the Pacific Railroad [probably in the Cole Junction area]. After a brief skirmish, the Confederates drove a Union cavalry force back into the city.

(Dr. Joseph S. Summers, Jr.)

A monument erected by the Winnie Davis Chapter of the Daughters of the Confederacy marked the location of the forward units of Price's army at Moreau Drive and Hough Park Road. This monument was moved in later years to the junction of Moreau Drive and Fairmont Boulevard.

Price Retreats

At dusk, dark clouds threatened rain. General Price, Old Pap to his men, rode about on his mount, Bucephalus, reassuring his men. By now, intelligence reports indicated that a large force of some 7,000 men and eight cannon under General Pleasonton were moving from St. Louis toward Jefferson City. A drizzling rain fell. The picket lines of opposing forces were so close that the men on both sides could see and hear each other. Ragged rifle fire continued throughout the night as young, untrained recruits fired in response to any provocation. Each braced for the tremendous struggle that would surely begin at dawn.

In a farmhouse belonging to the Wallendorf family in the Frog Hollow area, Price summoned his commanders. Much to the consternation of Governor Reynolds, Price and his staff mapped out plans and drafted orders for the next morning's retreat from Jefferson City. Reynolds gave vent to his frustrations and cursed the general's timidity and ineptness.

Before leaving Jefferson City, legend has it that Price paid $27.00 in Confederate currency for his room and board to the Wallendorfs. In later years, the Wallendorf family proudly displayed the walnut bed where General Price slept that night and a pistol left behind by a Confederate soldier. The down mattress the General slept on was probably a welcome relief from the rug he normally used in the field. The German food was also probably a welcome respite from field rations. It seems ironic that the German family extended its customary hospitality to its guest, knowing that they were opposed to the ideals and objectives for which the Confederate general was fighting. The house still stands, although extensively remodeled.

(George and Ruth Wallendorf)

BARTHOLOMEW WALLENDORF, SR. owned the house off Frog Hollow Road that General Sterling Price and his staff used as their headquarters.

(George and Ruth Wallendorf)

The Wallendorf residence, completed in 1860, was a two-story log structure commonly known as a dogtrot. This photograph taken in 1981 shows that the passageway between the two sides has been closed in and that exterior siding covers the logs. A kitchen has also been added. Tradition says that Price slept in the upper east room (the window covered with a board). The house is now owned by the Leon Beck family.

(George and Ruth Wallendorf)

According to the Wallendorf legend, Price slept in this four-poster bed. The bed was sold in 1981 to the Lonnie Wekenborg family.

OPPOSITE BELOW: Family legend says Price's troops killed all the livestock except one chicken that was hidden in the woods, and probably cleaned the springhouse of any edible goods. When the soldiers departed, exhausted horses were traded for fresh Wallendorf horses.

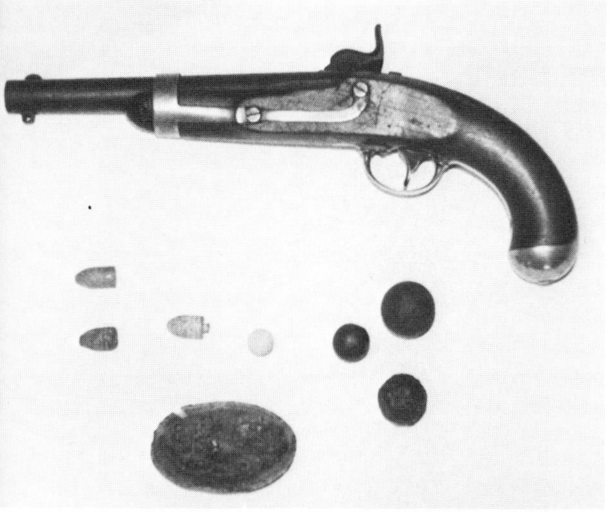

This muzzle-loading revolver, using a percussion cap, was found in a field on the Wallendorf farm and is owned by George Wallendorf. Also found were several Minié balls and round balls (possibly used in grape and canister), and a belt buckle with a U.S. insignia.

(George and Ruth Wallendorf)

(George and Ruth Wallendorf)

Echoes of the War

The circumstances of the Civil War affected many families in the Jefferson City area. In a few instances, homes were occupied by Union or Southern forces. In addition to the Dulle and Wallendorf residences (described in the text), the war touched several other homes and buildings in the area. Some are still standing. Documented evidence of many of the structures is difficult to find; however, in 1971, Boy Scout Troop No. 1 of the First United Methodist Church researched some of these buildings and the *Jefferson City News Tribune* wrote their stories.

The Bolton house was built in the mid 1830s at 1916 Green Berry Road by Dr. and Mrs. William Bolton, natives of North Carolina and Virginia, respectively. Considering the location of the house and the fact that forces on both sides occupied the banks of the Moreau River, a short distance to the south, it is highly likely that this house served as a stopping place for both armies. General Price's forces marched up Green Berry Road on October 6, 1864, following their crossing at Berry Springs. The home is now owned by Dr. and Mrs. Robert Johnston.

Vineyard Place at 1122 Moreau Drive, now owned by Mr. and Mrs. Nicholas Monaco, was built in the 1850s. In early October 1864, the high rooftop served as a lookout post over the Confederate lines marching up Green Berry Road and forming around the southern edge of the city.

Several homes along the area of Madison Street were occupied by Union Forces. Stories are told of how portholes were cut in the walls of the houses, and armed soldiers were stationed at each opening awaiting Price's 1864 arrival.

It is known that two churches were used as hospitals: the Second Baptist Church at 501 Monroe, where the benches were cut up for firewood; and the 1840 Episcopal Church on Madison Street, now the site of the city parking garage.

The home purchased by Gustavus Adolphus Parson in 1847 was built about 1830. Located at 105 Jackson, it was one of the many fine homes in the Adams, Jackson, High and Main Street area that served the Union army. This house was used as a hospital.

Why Price never attacked Jefferson City has long been the subject of speculation and controversy.

Did Price feel he lacked the strength to assault the city because he was the victim of bad intelligence and overestimated the strength of Federal forces? Price's later writing of his Missouri expedition was printed in *The Confederate Soldier of the Civil War:* ". . . and, after consultation with my general officers, I determined not to attack the enemy's entrenchments, as they outnumbered me nearly two to one and were strongly fortified . . ."

Or was it that fatal weakness of Southern temperament — that capacity for romantic sentimentality — that he could not bring himself to destroy a city he helped build, to kill helpless friends, or destroy the edifices where he had labored as a representative, speaker and governor?

Price also knew that a prolonged battle would certainly bring additional Union forces into the fray. He had little hope of remaining for any appreciable length of time in Jefferson City.

Was Price still shaken by his losses at Pilot Knob, and did not want to again subject his men to such losses?

Lastly, being a military man and not seeing the realization of mass uprisings and support he had hoped for against Federal dominaton, or the purported promise of new recruits, did he know that the Southern cause was doomed?

The slap of leather, the noisy cobbling of hooves, the clatter of rattling chains and traces, and the creaking of wagons filled the morning air in the gathering light of October as Price's cavalcade prepared to move out of Jefferson City. Upon hearing that the Confederate forces were departing Jefferson City, two Union cavalry regiments attacked the rear guard of Price's army commanded by Colonel J.A. Schnable. All day long, the Union cavalry under the command of General John B. Sandborn harassed Price's march, but the skirmishes were especially vicious in the Russellville area. The wounded from these skirmishes, along with those of the previous day, were taken to large homes on Dunklin and Jefferson Streets that were converted into hospitals.

Shelby's division of Price's army was again the lead division. They moved out smartly and headed for California, Missouri, where his troops burned the depot and a number of rail cars, and ransacked the city. Price's line of march was marked by the destruction of railroad lines, telegraph lines and bridges. He was aided in these endeavors by a number of guerrilla forces including Quantrill, Anderson and Todd. That morning, General Pleasonton arrived in Jefferson City to take command of the Union forces gathered there. While Pleasonton and his men rested, Price was being welcomed in Boonville with food, drink, supplies and ammunition. "Bloody Bill" Anderson rode into town with human scalps fluttering from his horse's bridle. Although General Price supposedly reacted with scorn, revulsion and disgust when the news of the Centralia massacre reached him, he met with Anderson at Boonville on October 11. Anderson was ordered to go back into north Missouri and destroy the North Missouri Railroad.

Pleasonton remained in Jefferson City to organize all the additional troops that would be arriving and to coordinate plans with General Rosecrans. General A.J. Smith's cavalry arrived in Jefferson City on October 14, followed on October 16 by Winslow's cavalry, and on October 17 nearly all General Mower's division arrived.

Meanwhile, Price left Boonville and headed for Kansas City. Battles ensued at both Glasgow and Sedalia. Straggling was a serious problem for marching men. The hard Missouri roads tortured bare and blistered feet. Price's army and the cumbersome wagon train were moving up the Missouri Valley one step ahead of the pursuing Federal cavalry under the command of General Sandborn. By the time Price's army was just past Boonville, Union cavalry forces were attacking the Confederate rear guard and pouncing on stragglers.

(State Historical Society of Missouri)

Guerrillas Pursued

Sensing the destination of Price's columns, Union cavalry set traps for the marauding guerrillas. An article in the August 20, 1864, *Harper's Weekly* reported: "It is believed that there are over 3,000 bushwhackers on the north side of the Missouri River. If this be true, the task of killing or expelling such a formidable body of thieves and murderers will be a huge one. The last anyone heard of Anderson's gang, who are reported to have done the damage on the Hannibal and St. Joseph Railroad, they were at Middle Grove, Monroe County, and were suppose to be pushing toward Chariton County. Five hundred Federal cavalry are in pursuit of them."

On October 21, George Todd was killed by a Union sniper about two miles northeast of Independence. He was buried in the Independence Cemetery.

On October 26, 1864, "Bloody Bill" Anderson and a number of his men were killed near Orrick in Ray County, about fifty miles northeast of Kansas City. A country woman had notified Union officers of Anderson's whereabouts. Shortly after noon, Anderson and over sixty of his men rode into an ambush, one of the many Union ambushes set up for the bushwhackers. Without hesitation, Anderson drew his gun and charged his enemy for the last time. The Federals found two dispatches on Anderson's body, one a special order which read, "Captain Anderson and his command, will at once proceed to the north side of the Missouri River, and permanently destroy the North Missouri Railroad, going as far east as practicable. He will report his operation at least every two days. By the order of Major General Price." Anderson's corpse was taken to Richmond, about ten miles northeast, and put on public display and photographed [picture not available at this printing]. Burial was without services in an unmarked grave in the Richmond Cemetery.

Battle of Westport

No longer could General Price command events, pick his objectives, and make the Union conform to his moves. Rather, his army was being hounded and mauled every step of the way.

On October 23, 1864, at Westport, near Kansas City, there was a battle subsequently described as "The Gettysburg of the West." Mauled, Price swung south with the Federal cavalry at his heels, and began a desperate retreat that ultimately took the tattered remnants of his command all the way to Arkansas. Fighting rearguard actions, a number of Price's officers and men were captured, among them General Marmaduke. By the time Price reached Confederate lines at Laynesport, Arkansas, in December, he had marched 1,454 miles and had lost 5,000 stands of arms, all of his artillery and most of his army. Governor Reynolds, still angry with Price's Jefferson City retreat, accused Price of "glaring mismanagement and distressing mental and physical military incapacity."

There was no further military threat to Jefferson City.

THIS IS THE SITE
OF THE DECISIVE
ENGAGEMENT IN
THE BATTLE OF WESTPORT
OCT. 23, 1864

(State Historical Society of Missouri)

The Westport battlefield monument in Loose Park, Kansas City, Missouri, marks the site of Price's final major defeat in Missouri. From here, Union forces pursued Price to Arkansas. A *Harper's Weekly* correspondent reported: "We are now rid of 20,000 or 30,000 half-starved bushwhackers and half-starved vagabonds, who, I hope, may never return to disturb the peaceful inhabitants north of the Arkansas River."

Part VI

1865

Slavery Abolished

On January 11, 1865, a constitutional convention assembled in St. Louis and overwhelmingly voted to abolish slavery within the state. There was a large celebration of the event in Jefferson City, culminating with Governor T.C. Fletcher addressing the throng at the Capitol. Thus, Missouri, by her own independent action, abolished slavery within her borders before the 13th amendment of the Constitution abolished it everywhere in the United States. That amendment was not adopted until December 1865 when the necessary number of states voted to put it into force.

THOMAS C. FLETCHER (1827-1899), Missouri's governor in 1865, signed the proclamation stating that slavery would be abolished in Missouri "now and forever."

(State Historical Society of Missouri)

AN ORDINANCE

ABOLISHING SLAVERY IN MISSOURI.

Be it ordained by the People of the State of Missouri, in Convention assembled:

That hereafter, in this State, there shall be neither slavery nor involuntary servitude, except in punishment of crime, whereof the party shall have been duly convicted; and all persons held to service or labor as slaves are hereby declared free.

Passed in Convention, January eleventh, A. D. one thousand eight hundred and sixty-five.

A. KREKEL, *President.*

CHAS. D. DRAKE, *Vice President.*

Three weeks before the Emancipation Proclamation was read by President Lincoln, 51 of the 66 members of the Missouri constitutional convention voted to abolish slavery in Missouri.

Over 110,000 Missouri slaves rejoiced at the news of their emancipation.

On April 9, 1865, Lee surrendered to Grant at Appomattox, Virginia. The joy of victory, solemn and triumphant, swept Jefferson City. The staunch ship of the Union had weathered a devastating storm. The most anciently rooted wrong had been corrected, but at a tremendous price of life and property. The Union had been preserved and the moral strengths and religious views that had been so bitterly contested would now be engendered, strengthened and allowed to grow so that man would be free, regardless of race, creed or color.

Missourians Ally With Mexico

Although the war was over, many Missourians, without waiting for their personal paroles, followed Generals Price and Shelby along with Governor Reynolds into Mexico to ally themselves with Emperor Maximilian. The Missourians settled in one of the largest Confederate colonies, Carlotta, named in honor of Maximilian's beautiful wife. While there, General Price's family joined him. When the revolutionaries backing Benito Juarez got the upperhand leading to the downfall of Maximilian's Empire, most of the Missouri colonists quit Mexico and headed back for Missouri. Generals Price and Shelby along with Governor Reynolds came back to Missouri in late 1866.

Two other Jefferson City residents were not so fortunate. Mosby Monroe Parsons, a lawyer and a State senator in charge of military appropriations, was a Confederate general who survived the war. It is reported he was the last Southern general to give up his command in Shreveport, Louisiana. He refused to take Drake's loyalty oath, and rode into Mexico with his brother-in-law, Austin Standish (also of Jefferson City). They were killed by bandits before Price or Shelby migrated to Mexico.

Part VII

Reconstruction

The Aftermath

The final chapter of the conflict that so severely rented the fabric of the nation was yet to be written. The full cumulative horror of the war — the dead, the wounded, the widows, the orphans — would impinge on the consciousness of Jefferson City and the nation. There were no U.S. institutions at the time to bring home the dead, and no compensation or dignity offered the wounded servicemen. Wives and children of the dead or wounded were regarded as irrelevant and allowed to make their own way. What appears to be a critical and retrospective assessment is tempered by what the nation and the good people of Jefferson City did in subsequent years.

For the wounded, the widows and the orphans of the servicemen, the churches of Jefferson City responded with Christian solicitude and reconciliation. In 1866, St. Peter's parish formed the St. Peter's Benevolent Society which was quickly staffed and funded to provide aid to those in need. Other churches and lodges followed suit. A number of Union disabled veterans were hired to work in state offices. However, many Confederate soldiers returned with a look of deep sadness and resignation; for having fought to the bitter miserable end, they found that they and their families were outcasts in a city they helped build. Many of their homes and lands had been appropriated by Union supporters, and they

(State Historical Society of Missouri)

To help the widows and orphans of the war, the St. Peter's Benevolent Society was formed. This organization continued in Jefferson City for many years.

had little recourse to recover them. The Drake Constitution, a tragic document of distrust, required a test oath which no former secessionist could sign as a qualification for suffrage. No person who had ever "given aid, comfort, countenance, or support to any person engaged in hostilities to the United States, or had ever by word or deed manifested his adherence to the cause of such enemies, or his desire for the triumph over the arms of the United States, or his sympathy with those engaged in exciting or carrying on the rebellion," was allowed to vote in any election in the state. The test oath was also required of clergymen. Father Jacob Miller (sometimes spelled Meller), the pastor of St. Peter's Church, refused to sign the oath stating that it was a violation of religious liberty guaranteed in the Constitution. Father Miller's refusal attracted wide attention in the city, and a number of state newspapers printed stinging invectives against the priest. Although threatened with arrest, the priest steadfastly refused to sign the oath. He continued to preach against the oath until it was finally eliminated in 1869.

Jefferson City benefited when soldiers decided to stay and settle in the city. The Burch brothers, Oscar G. and Nelson, were notable examples. They built homes with adjoining backyards at 924 Jefferson Street and 115 W. Atchison Street, respectively. In 1897, Oscar was a cashier at the First National Bank and Nelson was an abstractor. Their descendants were prominent in civic affairs for many years.

THE OATH OF LOYALTY

PRESCRIBED BY

THE CONSTITUTION, ADOPTED IN 1865.

I, Joseph W. McClurg do solemnly swear, that I am well acquainted with the terms of the third section of the second Article of the Constitution of the State of Missouri, adopted in the year eighteen hundred and sixty five, and have carefully considered the same; that I have never, directly or indirectly, done any of the acts in said section specified; that I have always been truly and loyally on the side of the United States against all enemies thereof, foreign and domestic; that I will bear true faith and allegiance to the United States, and will support the Constitution and laws thereof, as the supreme law of the land, any law or ordinance of any State to the contrary notwithstanding; that I will, to the best of my ability, protect and defend the Union of the United States, and not allow the same to be broken up and dissolved, or the Government thereof to be destroyed or overthrown, under any circumstances, if in my power to prevent it; that I will support the Constitution of the State of Missouri; and that I make this oath without any mental reservation or evasion, and hold it to be binding on me.

J. W. McClurg

Subscribed and sworn to before me this 23rd day of August 1866.

Thompson J Kelly Clerk of County Court, By T. Kelly Deputy

(State Historical Society of Missouri)

The "Ironclad Oath" was part of the Missouri Constitution of 1865. Written by Charles Drake, it required that anyone registering to vote had to take an oath that they had never helped the enemy [the South] in any way. The Oath of Loyalty was repealed by an amendment in 1870.

Many of the farmers chased from their homes by bushwhackers during the Civil War, in places like Russellville, Wardsville, Lohman and surrounding areas, also decided to stay in Jefferson City. In the next ten years, Jefferson City experienced a building boom that doubled its population. Jefferson City's streets were paved, a new high school was constructed, a new gas plant was erected, and the streets were illuminated at night by coal-oil lamps perched atop wooden poles. Industries began to spring up in the southwest and in the Mill Bottom area.

The reestablishment of an effective state government was made difficult because many of the state's records had been lost, destroyed or never returned. Of special concern was the loss of the secretary of state's land records, along with the state auditor's tax records. Much property had changed hands or had been expropriated during the war.

Black soldiers, many of them ex-slaves recruited from Missouri to serve with the Union forces, made up the Sixty-second and Sixty-fifth Colored Infantries. They served as "camp laborers" digging trenches and fortifications primarily in Louisiana and Texas. When the war ended, troops from these units donated part of their salaries to the formation of an institute designed to benefit freed slaves. It was to be located in Missouri, and the institute was to combine a study and labor curriculum. On June 25, 1866, incorporating papers were filed in the Circuit Court of Cole County. On September 14, 1866, Lincoln Institute in Jefferson City opened its doors to two students. There were a number of drives for funds to sustain and expand the Institute. A history of Lincoln University reveals that on two occasions Jesse James, the outlaw, contributed funds to the Institute.

(1900 Illustrated Sketch Book)

Lincoln Institute, now Lincoln University, was opened in 1866 with two students attending. The determination and commitment of the officers and soldiers of the 62nd and 65th U.S. colored infantry made this institution of higher learning a reality.

The Care of the Dead

(State Historical Society of Missouri)

During the Civil War, soldiers were buried on the farms and fields where they fell. Wounded were placed aboard wagons to be transported to the nearest hospital. During frequent halts, the wagons were cleared of the wounded who had died. While the wagons continued on to their destinations, officers and enlisted men alike were buried in nameless graves along the roadside. At the conclusion of the War, over a million graves of servicemen were scattered throughout the United States. A national cemetery program was started, and Jefferson City was selected as one of the sites. Remains were removed from battlefields at Boonville, Sedalia, Warrensburg, Glasgow, Brunswick and from the fields, farms and roadsides of Cole, Callaway, Boone, and other nearby counties, and reinterred in the National Cemetery.

The national cemeteries were designed to offer perpetual testimony of the concern of a grateful nation that the lives and services of members of the armed forces, who served their nation well, would be appropriately commemorated. The flag of the United States was to be flown proudly, the grounds and headstones were to be well-tended, and an air of dedication and serenity was to be maintained. At a number of cemeteries, a plaque with the Gettysburg Address can be seen. At others, the following poem:

> On Fame's eternal camping ground
> Their silent tents are spread
> And Glory guards, with solemn round
> The bivouac of the dead.

As one veteran aptly put it, "the wound was closed but it would take a long time to heal."

(Dr. Joseph S. Summers,

On July 17, 1862, President Lincoln signed an act authorizing the establishment of national cemeteries. The first burial at the site of the National Cemetery in Jefferson City was in 1861, when an unknown Civil War soldier was interred. In 1867 this site on East McCarty Street was declared a National Cemetery.

Epilogue

Although Union General Thomas L. Price of Jefferson City and Confederate General Sterling Price were adversaries during the Civil War, their families were joined when Celsus Price, son of Sterling Price, married Celeste Price, daughter of General Thomas Price. General Sterling Price, broken in health and spirit, died in St. Louis on September 29, 1867.

In the mid 1870s, President Arthur named ex-Lieutenant Governor Thomas Reynolds to investigate relations with Latin American nations. Reynolds was an accomplished linguist. Before he could make the voyage, a great tragedy struck. A spark from a fireplace fire ignited his wife's nightgown and she later died from the burns. In the late 1880s, Reynolds' health began to deteriorate, and he worried that he would become a burden to his new wife. On March 30, 1887, his body was found at the bottom of a St. Louis elevator shaft. Historians still ponder whether he jumped or fell the 80 feet to his death.

President Lincoln eventually split with the Blairs and demanded Postmaster General Montgomery Blair's resignation. Frank Blair, Jr., advanced to the rank of major general in the Union army and commanded a unit at Vicksburg. After the War in 1868, he was the unsuccessful vice-presidential nominee on the Democratic ticket, but later formed a dynasty that dominated Missouri politics for years. He died of a paralytic stroke in 1875.

After resigning his Shenandoah Valley Command in June 1862, Fremont went to New York and prepared to oppose Lincoln as Republican presidential nominee in 1864. He was disappointed that not a single leading Republican endorsed his candidacy.

For all his honors and accomplishments with the Union cavalry, after the war General Pleasonton was offered the permanent rank of lieutenant colonel; not in the cavalry he loved, but in the infantry. He resigned and went into railroading.

(Dr. Joseph S. Summers, Jr.)

(Dr. Joseph S. Summers, Jr.)

FACING PAGE AND LEFT: John S. Marmaduke was serving as Missouri's governor when he died in 1887. A monument stands in his honor at the Woodland Cemetery on East McCarty Street in Jefferson City, where he was interred.

General John Sappington Marmaduke was elected Governor of Missouri in November 1884. Although still a bachelor, he was known for his tender solicitude toward children, and his Christmas parties for children at the Executive Mansion were eagerly anticipated by the children of Jefferson City. In 1887, he died the day before the Christmas party was to be held. The weather was so bad that he was buried in the Woodland Cemetery in Jefferson City instead of the family burial plot in Arrow Rock. A large granite obelisk with the inscription "He Was Fearless and Incorruptible" marks his grave.

Increate with military honors, General Grant became President, but his administration was wracked with graft, corruption, inefficiency and fraud. After leaving office, Grant fell heavily into debt from bad investments. He also suffered from throat cancer caused by smoking at least 20 cigars a day. Ulysses S. Grant died on July 23, 1885.

The Governor of Missouri, Thomas Crittenden, offered a reward of $10,000 each for the delivery and conviction of Jesse and Frank James. Charles and Robert Ford were staying with Jesse and Lee and their family in St. Joseph. On April 3, 1882, Robert Ford shot Jesse James in the back of the head as he stepped on a chair to straighten a picture. The Ford brothers pleaded guilty to the charge of murder, were sentenced to be hanged, and sent to the Jefferson City penitentiary. Governor Crittenden gave the Ford brothers an unconditional pardon, causing a howl of protest from the citizens of Missouri. Criticism of the pardon did not subside and ended the governor's brilliant political career.

Frank James was living a sequestered life in Baltimore when he read about the pardon and, fearing assassination himself, hastened to Jefferson City. On October 4, 1884, he stayed the night in the McCarty Hotel. With James was John N. Edwards, the newspaper editor who had always defended Frank and Jessie because of their friendship during the Civil War. They registered under the names Jno. Edwards, Sedalia, and B. F. Winfrey, Marshall, Missouri. The following day arrangements with Governor Crittenden were completed, the initital contact having been made by a letter from

(State Historical Society of Missouri)

JESSE WOODSON JAMES (1847-1882) joined the Confederate forces at the age of 17. He later made a name for himself as an outlaw. Missouri history books abound with legends of his exploits.

ROBERT FORD (below right) and CHARLES FORD (below left) confessed to the murder of Jesse James. Less than one year later, Governor Crittenden pardoned the brothers.

(State Historical Society of Missouri)

(State Historical Society of Missouri)

Frank to the governor mailed from St. Louis on September 30. Shortly before five that afternoon, Governor Crittenden assembled several state officials and some newsmen in his office. He read the letter, and as they were discussing it, Edwards and James entered the room. Frank handed the governor his pistol and cartridge belt saying, "Governor Crittenden, I want to hand over to you that which no other living man has been permitted to touch since 1861, and to say that I am your prisoner."

He was committed to the Jackson County jail at Independence for trial. During the weeks in the Jackson County jail, there were newspaper articles written in his defense. He was welcomed by a stream of old friends and many gifts were bestowed upon him. Jackson County Prosecutor Wallace dismissed the charges against Frank James in January 1883. James was then sent to the jail at Gallatin to face charges of bank robbery, train robbery and murder. Because of these charges, Governor Crittenden refused the January 1883 request of the Governor of Minnesota to remove Frank James to that state. Following a much-publicized trial in Gallatin, the jury found the defendant not guilty in September 1883. Frank James turned respectable and was honored in later life for his part in the Confederate cause. Because there was so much criticism of the manner in which the Ford brothers killed Jesse James and the subsequent pardon, a despondent Charles Ford committed suicide less than a year after Jesse James was killed.

(State Historical Society of Missouri)

ALEXANDER FRANKLIN (FRANK) JAMES (1843-1915), older brother of Jesse James, was a member of the Confederate army and rode with Quantrill's guerrillas. Two years after the murder of his brother, Frank turned himself in to face charges of train and bank robbery. He was exonerated. The closing years of his life were spent quietly on a farm in Clay County, Missouri.

Quantrill hand-picked a group of his best men and headed for Washington to assassinate President Lincoln. John Wilkes Booth beat him to it, and on May 10, 1865, Quantrill was shot down by Federal marshals in Spencer County, Kentucky. Quantrill left all his money to his girlfriend who promptly used it to start a brothel in St. Louis.

When "Bloody Bill" Anderson was killed [see pg. 130], he was carrying approximately $600, six pistols and several watches. Anderson's horse, along with his pistols and watches, were given as "honorable trophies" to the Union officers who killed him.

"Wild Bill" Hickok became marshal of several Kansas towns, gunning down a number of desperados before being gunned down himself at Deadwood, Dakota Territory.

After his capture at the Battle of Lexington and subsequent release by General Price, Colonel James Mulligan was placed in command of the Baltimore and Ohio Railroad in western Virginia. He fought in a number of skirmishes, and during the Battle of Winchester, Virginia, was mortally wounded. His brother-in-law, while attempting to carry him from the field, was also fatally shot. President Lincoln granted a posthumous commission of Brevet Brigadier General for Colonel Mulligan "for gallant and meritorious services at the Battle of Winchester."

WILLIAM FREDERICK (BUFFALO BILL) CODY (1846-1917) served in the 7th Regiment of Kansas cavalry during the Civil War. He is well known for his many adventures as a Pony Express rider, scout and guide for the U. S. Army, state Representative from Nebraska, and eventually the organizer of his "Wild West Show" that became the hit of continents.

(State Historical Society of Missouri)

During the Civil War reinterment program, only 58 percent of the dead could be identified. Of the 653 Civil War dead buried in the Jefferson City National Cemetery, there are 331 known Union dead, 313 unknown Union dead, and nine Rebel soldiers or citizens. The U.S. Army decided that something should be done in future wars to permit better identification of the dead and notification of the next of kin. Two circular tags were devised, and are worn by all military personnel. In the event of death, one of the tags remains with the body and the other is used to notify the next of kin. Today, all military men know them as "dog tags."

* * * * * *

Because of its political significance and strategic location, Jefferson City was indeed a military and political prize actively contested by both Union and Confederate forces. We are mindful that men fought and died attacking or defending the city. As we walk about Jefferson City, we are reminded of the sacrifices made to preserve the Union and of the fact that we are walking on hallowed ground.

OVERLEAF: Bird's Eye View of Jefferson City. The sketch by Prof. Rugu of Chicago depicts the capital city in 1869. Having sustained little, if any, damage during the Civil War, Jefferson City continued to flourish.

(Mr. and Mrs. F. Joe DeLong, II)

JACKSON ST.
ADAMS ST.
MONROE ST.
MARSHALL ST.
WATER ST.
7 MARKET HOUSE.
8 FEMALE COLLEGE.
9. PUBLIC SCHOOL.
10 R.R DEPOT
11. FAIR GROUND.
THE CAPITOL

JEFFERSON ST
WASHINGTON ST
ELM ST
BROADWAY
HIGH ST
HARRISON ST
CLAY ST
VIEW
OF
CITY
CHURCHES.
13 EPISCOPAL
METHODIST
LUTHERAN
COURT & MARKET HOUSE

Bibliography

Anderson, Galusha. *The Story of a Border City During the Civil War.* Boston: Little Brown & Company, 1908.

Backes, Raymond C. *Catholicism in Capital City, 1813-1928.* St. Paul: St. Paul Seminary, 1956.

Battles and Leaders of the Civil War. Vol. 1, 2. New York: Thomas Yoseloff, Inc., 1956.

Baysinger, Don et al. "Scouts Develop Historic Trail." *The Sunday News and Tribune*, Jefferson City, Missouri, 18 April 1971.

Boyd, James P. *Military and Civil Life of Gen. Ulysses S. Grant.* Philadelphia: P.W. Ziegler & Company, 1885.

Brownlee, Richard S. *Gray Ghosts of the Confederacy.* Baton Rouge, La.: Louisiana State University Press, 1958.

Burch, John P. *Charles W. Quantrill.* Vega, Texas: John P. Burch, 1923.

Castel, Albert. *General Sterling Price and the Civil War in the West.* Baton Rouge: Louisiana State University Press, 1968.

Castel, Albert. *William Clarke Quantrill, His Life and Times.* New York: Frederick Fell, Inc., 1962.

Catton, Bruce. *Grant Moves South.* Boston: Little Brown and Co., 1960.

Civil War Maps In The National Archives. The National Archives and Records Service, Washington, 1964.

"The Civil War: Jefferson City, A City Divided." *Post Tribune*: Jefferson City, 14-17 July 1985.

Civil War Times. Gettysburg, Pa.: Historical Times, Inc., 1973.

Cole County Cooking and Culture. Jefferson City: Bicentennial Commission, 1976.

Conroy, Sarah Booth. "Remembering Ulysses S. Grant." *Washington Post*: Washington, D.C., 23 July 1985.

Davis, Walter Bickford and Daniel S. Durrie. *An Illustrated History of Missouri.* Cincinnati: A. J. Hall and Company, 1876.

Edom, Clifton C. *Missouri Sketch Book.* Columbia: Lucas Brothers Publishing, 1963.

Edwards, John. *Shelby and His Men or The War in the West.* Cincinnati: Miami Printing and Publishing Co., 1867.

The Encyclopedia Britannica. 14th ed., New York: Encyclopedia Britannica, Inc., 1938.

Fitzgerald, Tom. "A Raid on Centralia." *The Missouri Statesman*: Columbia, 30 September 1864.

Foote, Shelby. *The Civil War, A Narrative.* New York: Random House, 1963.

Ford, James E. *History of Jefferson City.* Jefferson City: The New Day Press, 1938.

Grant, Ulysses. *Personal Memoirs of U.S. Grant.* Vol. 1. New York: Charles L. Webster & Co., 1885.

Grisham, Howard C. *The Centralia Massacre, September 27, 1864.* Jefferson City: Howard C. Grisham, 1964.

Harding, Samuel B. *Missouri Party Struggles in the Civil War Period.* American Historical Association, Washington: Government Printing Office, 1901.

Harper's Pictorial History. New York: Harper and Brothers, 1866.

Harper's Weekly. New York: Harper & Brothers, 1862 and 1864.

Harrison, Samuel F. *History of Hermann, Missouri.* Historic Hermann, Inc. 1966.

Hinton, Richard J. *Rebel Invasion of Missouri and Kansas.* Chicago: Church and Goodman, 1865.

Hokombe and Adams. *An Account of the Battle of Wilson's Creek.* Springfield, Mo.: The Greene County Historical Society and the Springfield Public Library, 1961.

Humorous and Pathetic Stories of Abraham Lincoln. Fort Wayne, Indiana: The Lincoln Publishing Company.

Knipp, Gloria (ed.). *Tipton, A History of the Community.* Tipton: The Tipton Bicentennial Committee, 1976.

Lee, Robert E. et al. *The Confederate Soldier in the Civil War.* Fairfax Press.

Lewis, Lloyd. *Captain Sam Grant.* Boston: Little Brown & Co., 1950.

March, David D. *The History of Missouri.* New York: Lewis Historical Publishing Company, 1967.

Marshall, Albert P. *Soldiers' Dream.* Jefferson City: Lincoln University, 1966.

Meyer, Duane G. *The Heritage of Missouri.* St. Louis: River City Publishers, 1982.

Monaghan, Jay. *Civil War on the Western Border, 1854-1865.* New York: Bonanza Books, 1956.

The National Cemetery, Jefferson City, Missouri, 1861-1981. Jefferson City: Mid-Missouri Geneological Society, Inc., 1981.

O'Flaherty, Daniel. *General Jo Shelby, Undefeated Rebel.* Chapel Hill: The University of North Carolina Press, 1954.

Ohman, Marian M. *The History of Missouri Capitols.* Columbia: University of Missouri, 1982.

Ordinances of the City of Jefferson, 1859. Jefferson City, Mo.

Parrish, William E. *A History of Missouri.* Columbia: University of Missouri Press, 1973.

Rea, Ralph R. *Sterling Price, The Lee of the West.* Little Rock: Pioneer Press, 1959.

Rice, Herb. "Bold Missouri Editor Rode With Jo Shelby." *The Kansas City Times*, 24 October 1961.

Savage, W. Sherman. *The History of Lincoln University.* Jefferson City: Lincoln University, 1939.

Scrivner, Charles Lee. "Benjamin Payne Scrivner and the 7th Missouri State Militia Calvary." *Pioneer Times*: Jefferson City, April 1984.

Settle, William A., Jr. *Jesse James Was His Name.* Lincoln: University of Nebraska Press, 1977.

Shoemaker, Floyd C. *Missouri and Missourians.* Chicago: Lewis Publishing Co., 1943.

Shrader, Dorothy H. *Hermann Sesquicentennial.* Hermann, Mo.: Graf Printing Co., 1986.

Sone, Guy M. *Major General John Charles Fremont's Camp Lillie in Jefferson City, Missouri 1861*. Jefferson City: 1961

Stevens, Walter B. *The Centennial History of Missouri.* St. Louis: The S. J. Clarke Publishing Company, 1921.

Summers, Joseph S., Jr. *Pictorial Folk History of Jefferson City, Missouri 1890-1900.* Jefferson City: Summers Publishing, 1982.

U.S. Army, Adjutant General's Office. *Official Army Register of the Volunteer Force of the United States Army for the Years 1861, 62, 63, 64, 65.* Washington: Adjutant General's Office, July 1867.

U.S. Army. *Report of the Quartermaster General to the Secretary of War for the Year 1868.* Washington: Government Printing Office, 1868.

U.S. Army Quartermaster General's Office. *Roll of Honor, Names of Soldiers Who Died in the Defense of the American Union.* Washington: Government Printing Office, 1869.

U.S. Army, Quartermaster General's Office. *Statement of the Disposition of Some of the Bodies of Union Soldiers and Prisoners of War Whose Remains Have Been Removed to National Cemeteries.* Washington: Government Printing Office, 1868.

Veterans Administration. *Development of the National Cemetery System.* Washington: Veterans Administration, January 15, 1978.

Viles, Jonas. *Lessons To Be Drawn From the Fire in the State Capitol, Jefferson City.* American Historical Association, Washington: Government Printing Office, 1911.

Violette, Eugene Morrow. *A History of Missouri.* Boston: D.C. Heath & Co., Publishers, 1918.

Wakelyn, Jon L. *Biographical Dictionary of the Confederacy*. Westport, Ct.: Greenwood Press, 1977.

Wiley, Bell Irvin. *The Common Soldier in the Civil War.* New York: Gosset & Dunlap,1951.

Williams, Walter. *The State of Missouri.* Columbia: Press of E. W. Stephens, 1904.

About The Author

Dino A. Brugioni was born at Bevier, Missouri, where he attended grade school. A graduate of the Jefferson City High School, he is the Jefferson City High School Alumni Association's 1980 recipient of the Distinguished Alumni Award. He is also a graduate of the Jefferson City Junior College.

During World War II, Mr. Brugioni flew in 66 bombardment and a number of reconnaissance missions over North Africa, Italy, France, Germany and Yugoslavia. He was awarded the Purple Heart, the Air Medal with eight oak leaf clusters and a Presidential Unit Citation. After the War, he earned B.A. and M.A. degrees from George Washington University in Washington, D.C.

In 1948, Mr. Brugioni joined the Central Intelligence Agency and became an expert on industrial installations in the Soviet Union. This experience, along with his knowledge of reconnaissance, led to his selection as a member of a cadre of founding officers of the National Photographic Interpretation Center in Washington. As a senior officer at the Center, he directed the exploitation of sensitive aerial photography taken during crisis situations. He received numerous citations and several medals for his intelligence work, but is especially proud of the commendation received from President Kennedy for his performance during the Cuban Missile

Crisis of October 1962. Recently, he was awarded the prestigious Pioneer in Space medal by the U.S. Government for his work in space reconnaissance.

In 1982, Mr. Brugioni retired as a senior official and an aerial reconnaissance and photo interpretation expert for the Central Intelligence Agency.

Mr. Brugioni has written extensively on the application of aerial photography to intelligence and other fields and has won a number of writing awards for these endeavors. It was while researching and writing an article for the *Smithsonian Magazine* that he found numerous references to Jefferson City during the Civil War. He decided to pursue further research at the Library of Congress, the National Archives, the Veterans Administration and other repositories for more information of his home town during this critical period.

The Civil War in Missouri as Seen From the Capital City is the result of that research.